KEY ACCOUNT
SELLING

KEY ACCOUNT SELLING.

New Strategies for
Maximizing Profit and Penetration

MACK HANAN

AMERICAN MANAGEMENT ASSOCIATIONS

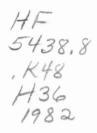
Library of Congress Cataloging in Publication Data

Hanan, Mack.
    Key account selling.

    Includes index.
    1. Selling—Key accounts. I. Title.
HF5438.8.K48H36   1982   658.8'105   82-71307
ISBN 0-8144-5751-7

First Printing

To Paula Brown and her key account teams,

who have done more than all but one man to make AT&T a competitive force by driving dozens of top-tier customers, scores of business function systems, and millions of profit dollars with these strategies.

Preface

Two strategies will principally determine profits on sales through the year 2000. One is to structure the sales force along two-tier lines. The other is to concentrate money and human resources at the top tier of upper management decision makers, where key account selling takes place.

In an increasing number of industries, the mass movement of products on a price-performance basis has become obsolete as a major profit source. The combination of increasing sales costs and shrinking margins has made selling on the bottom tier progressively cost-ineffective for many major companies. Sellers can no longer afford complete market coverage with complete product lines, selling tonnage or gallonage to anyone and everyone, even at breakeven prices. The sales function can no longer afford to work for the manufacturing process. Nor can the sales function continue to subsidize platoons of vendor sales representatives who practice ill-named "professional selling skills" in an attempt to establish distinctions without a difference between their commodity-type offerings and the virtually identical commodity offerings of direct competitors.

Bottom-tier selling is price selling. It is high-cost, low-margin selling. It is adversary selling, pitting the aggressive persuasiveness of self-seeking product differentiators against the self-seeking defensiveness of purchasers. Only one can win—at least until the next time.

Approximately 80 percent of most companies' sales volume takes place in this basement tier of the sales process. Yet it only accounts for as little as 20 percent or less of all profits.

The upper tier is another world. Here, 20 percent or so of a company's total volume can contribute as much as 80 percent of profits on sales. This is the arena of key account selling. It is the make-or-break part of the sales function.

Top-tier selling is value-based selling. No products, services, or systems are sold—only the dollar value of the bottom-line impact they can make on a customer's business. Asking price is directly correlated with the customer's added value, enabling margins to be high when customer value is high. Sellers and buyers consult on how the values can be implemented. They share their mutual knowledge of the customer's business problems that they can solve together and the opportunities they can help achieve. They partner with each other. Consequently, both win new knowledge, new opportunity to implement it, and new profits. Both seek a common objective: to improve customer profit. The customer's earnings and the seller's margins ride on it.

In the 1980–2000 generation, growth—to say nothing of survival—will depend on how well businesses in every industry can manage the 20 percent of their sales functions that contribute 80 percent of their profits—their top-tier key account sales forces. Companies that continue to play the two-tier game by universally applying the vendor selling tactics of the bottom tier will perish.

How can we be so sure?

Throughout the current generation—1960–1980—The Greenhouse Group has concentrated on top-tier selling as a major corporate growth strategy. We have studied and popularized the two-tier concept. We have advocated the creation of a doctrine for key account selling that is separate and distinct from vendor selling. We have counseled the establishment of a separate sales force that is deliberately recruited, trained, and managed to execute the doctrine. We have given the name *consultative selling* to our doctrine. We have written the book on it. Today, thousands of key account sales representatives in hundreds of companies in dozens of industries go by the book. They position themselves in a consultative capacity with high-level decision makers. They become partners in improving customer profits in return for high margins.

These trained consultative sales representatives regularly demolish competitiors who try to neutralize them with traditional vendor selling skills. When they have technically superior products and sell them in a consultative, profit-improving manner, it is a walkover. Even when they have only parity products, they almost always prevail. But neither of these is the acid test. What has been the result when their products are technically surpassed by competition—what then? Whenever they are able to demonstrate a superior profit for the customer, or a similar profit that is quicker in coming on stream or is surer, consultative selling gives them the crucial advantage.

Sometimes we have been surprised at these results, which defy vendor logic. Sometimes, too, the consultative representatives who make the sales have admitted their own surprise. But their customers have not been surprised. They know what their needs are. They know that it is profit, not products, that they must acquire. What benefit, they ask, is a supplier's technical superiority unless it can be translated into customer profit superiority? We don't want your technology, they say.

That is your cost. We want its impact on our business. That is our profit.

Our doctrine of consultative selling has evolved, as all doctrines must, through practical application. We have taught the skills, monitored their implementation, and audited the outcomes. If there were a Latin proverb to synthesize what we have done, it would be "From many experiences, one expertise."

At the leading edge of what we have learned is the discovery that consultative selling skills are one-third of a comprehensive key account penetration system. As we now practice it, two supportive strategies bracket it on either side. The first is an industry-dedicated key account data base. It acts as a computerized proposal partner to a consultative sales representative. We have given the sales representative's new partner a name. We call it APACHE, an acronym for *A*ccount *P*enetration *a*t *C*ustomer *H*igh Levels of *E*ntry. The key account sales representatives and their APACHE partners will be the selling superteam of the next 20 years.

The second strategy to support our consultative penetration approach is a key account planning process on an account-by-account basis, treating each major customer as an individual market. Along with the planning strategy is an audit procedure to make certain that opportunity is being maximized and that, conversely, no major opportunities are being left open to competitive inroads.

Consultative selling, customer data basing, and an account penetration planning process—these are the three interlocking components of our key account penetration system. They create what we like to think of as a minimal system: They provide everything you need, but no more, to make the maximum penetration into your key sources of profitable sales.

MACK HANAN

Contents

1

Concentration and Dedication

There are three rules for increasing profits on sales. Rule one is to concentrate on penetrating your key accounts. Rule two is to concentrate more. Rule three is to concentrate even more again. To use a generalization, if less than 80 percent of your management time and talent, your sales planning, your operational funding, and your coaching and counseling is being dedicated to growing your key account business—both existing and prospects—you are not concentrating.

If you have not been concentrating, you have been in good company—good, that is, in terms of major corporations in mainstream industries. For the most part, the *Fortune* 500 has favored a monolithic sales strategy. Every sales representative calls on some key accounts. Every product is sold in the same way based on price performance, whether the customer is a key account or not. This is called professional selling. It is also called price selling, and there is very little that is professional about it. There is also very little that is unusually profitable.

The heyday of monolithic sales organizations is over. The costs of volume—of making it, warehousing it, selling it, and doing all the paperwork it requires, including collecting on it—have outrun the profits. Cost inflation is one pincer of the profit squeeze. The other is price erosion. As costs go up and prices go down under standardized, homogenized competition, sales are often made more for their contribution to manufacturing cost than to profit. Sales support manufacturing instead of the other way around.

There is a place for price-performance selling, or vendor selling. The proper location is at the purchasing function level, whatever it may be named in your industry. This is the level that issues requests for proposals, defines specifications, and invites bids whose sole significant deviation from each other will most likely be in price. If you have mature products, services, or systems whose performance is more or less replicated by competition, they should be vended as commodities in the least costly manner. These transactions flow across the basement tier of a two-tier sales environment.

To be unusually profitable, you must concentrate on the top tier. That is where the profits are. In most cases, they are underexploited. It is safe to say that whatever your current profits from key account sales may amount to, they are probably undervalued by one-third to two-thirds of their potential. If this estimate seems high, reduce it by half. If it still seems high, halve it further. It is still a formidable opportunity, the equivalent of developing a new growth market. Yet it offers far fewer risks than a new market and far more cost-effective rewards.

The risk-reward ratio of key account selling is so unusually favorable because of one unique attribute. We define a key account as a customer whose profits you can improve significantly through the premium value delivered by what you sell—at the same time your own profits are significantly improved by the premium price you can receive in return. As a result, key account customers wants you to sell to them whenever you can demonstrate your ability to improve their profits. If you do not fully capitalize on your sales opportunity, you deprive the customer of added profits. In consultative selling, customer sales insistence takes the place of sales resistance.

No less risky strategy for profit growth exists than key account concentration. No greater opportunity to profit from sales exists than maximizing top-tier penetration. Nor is there a business growth strategy that is more certain or more capable of quick payoff.

Knowing the Customer's Business

The top tier, where key account selling must take place, refuses vendor tactics. It is unresponsive to feature and benefit comparisons. It stares glassy-eyed at laundry lists of ingredients, components, formulas, subsystems, process variations, or ever more inclusive warrantees. It ignores price as a reason to buy, resists the bait of a trial close, and does not take kindly to having its objections overcome. From its perspective, professional selling is amateurish selling. It deals with vendors simply by declining to deal with them.

Companies that do not respect two-tier selling always ask how they can "sell up": "How can we get our sales representatives to be able to stand before a top-level decision maker?" They ask the wrong question. Any vendor may make it to the top once. The right question is: "How can we get our representatives invited back a second time?" Unless that happens, no new knowledge of the customer's business will flow to them. No decisions to buy will flow to them either.

How can your key account representatives be invited back? There is only one way. On their first call, they must present new knowledge of improving the customer's business—not knowledge of the representatives' business, not product or process knowledge, not knowledge of your latest terms, conditions, or deals but knowledge of the customer's own business. This is the crucial difference between top-tier and bottom-tier selling. The bottom tier wants to hear about your business. The top tier wants only to learn more about its own.

Concentrating on key account penetration inescapably means concentrating on knowing the businesses of your key accounts. It means knowing customer problems and the dollar values of those problems. It means knowing customer opportunities and the dollar values of those opportunities. It means knowing how you can help solve the problems and help achieve the opportunities. It means knowing the dollar values of your solutions. It means bringing this information into your business in the form of a key account data base and positioning the data base as the foundation of your key account penetration.

Key account selling is information-intensive. To say the same thing in another way, it is data-dependent. In order to "have the goods" in top-tier salesmanship, it is not enough to have the product. You must have the customer knowledge that will let you know what financial impact that product will make on a customer's business. The dimensions of this added dollar value are the sum and substance of the dialogs your key account representatives must have with high-level customer decision makers. Otherwise, they will be talking to themselves about themselves: an audience of one but a market of none.

Managing from Customer Data

The decision to concentrate on key account selling as the bull's-eye of your sales management is, first of all, a decision to manage from a base of customer data, not products. It puts you in the information business. It acknowledges your recognition of the central fact about top-tier selling. For both seller and buyer, information makes up 90 percent of every transaction. Nothing moves until the information moves.

Knowledge of how to improve their businesses is the principal element in any sale to key account customers. It possesses reality because it is their business. Nothing, including your physical ironware, is as real for them as that. When you talk about your products, you may think you are discussing tangibles if they have weight, size and shape, texture, color, or aroma. But these are simple bits and pieces of information. They become real only when you can connect them to the reality of the customer's business by showing the financial values they will deliver. In this way of looking at things, only financial values, not products, are tangible.

As manager of this type of information-transfer business, you will preside over a structure to organize customer data, a method to bring new data into the structure, and a system to let your key account sales force gain access to the data. Our APACHE-type structure is designed to meet these needs. It stores customer data by the divisions or departments you sell to, by the functions within them, and by the individual problems and opportunities within the functions. It also stores your solutions to each problem and opportunity, expressed both as product and service systems and in terms of their financial effect on the customer's business. By using their APACHE data system to mix and match your solutions with customer problems, your key account representatives can come up with the optimal solution based on improved profit for both you and their accounts.

An APACHE-type data system is the consultative representatives' proposal partner. Together, they develop each proposal. Until your representatives arrive at their optimal solution, they can play "What if . . .?" games with APACHE. What if we propose this solution—what profit opportunity will it give the customer? What will it give us? What if we alter this module, this component, this piece of equipment, this service? What then? What is the best solution?

Key account consultants and their APACHE proposal partner are the nucleus of your inside top-tier sales team. When they go outside to sell, the sales representatives may be supported by technical, service, financial, and other resource teams who will implement their solution on the customer's premises. But at home—and this can be literally at the sales representatives' own homes if they are equipped with portable minicomputers—they and their APACHE can control each account by the amount of improved profits they propose for it every year.

Operating as a Financial Service Business

When you decide to concentrate on the penetration of your top-tier business opportunity, you give up the familiar positioning of your traditional business. If you currently define the nature of your business in product terms, you will lose it. If the definition of your business is based on its raw materials or its processes, you will lose it, too. So it will be with any definition that has to do with your own business instead of your relationship to the businesses of your key accounts. From the customer's perspective, which must now become your own, your business is always defined as a financial service business whose product is improved customer profit.

Financial service businesses are information businesses. They are businesses that deal with information about monetary values. They are personal service businesses that act as stewards of their customers' financial well-being. They consult on the most cost-effective strategies for appreciating each customer's current worth. They are evaluated by results that appear in black and white on the customer's bottom line. Were profits improved? Were they improved as much as promised? Could they have been improved even more? Could they have been improved even faster? Will they continue to be improved? Can someone else improve them more?

How consultative is each of your key account representatives? Their report cards are contained in their customers' answers to these questions. What about the age-old question, can they sell? Unless the other questions can be answered positively by their customers, selling—in the vendor mode of price-performance product comparisons—may be the worst thing that top-tier sales representatives can do.

Your key account representatives must position themselves as financial service representatives. This does not mean they sell a financial service. It means they provide one. The name of the service is improved profitability for their customers. If your business has a strong product heritage, it may be initially difficult for your representatives to reposition their offerings from hardware to hard dollars; from something that goes into a customer's business to something that comes out of its improved operation; from something that is mature and

stale to something that is always fresh and welcome—
and often all too rare.

If you are in the electronic data processing business,
your representatives will have to learn how to sell the
improved profits resulting from solving a customer's
problems through data processing rather than from vending an EDP system itself.

If you are a materials cleaning machinery manufacturer, your representatives will have to learn how to sell
the improved profits resulting from solving a customer's
problems through materials cleaning rather than from
vending cleaning equipment itself.

If you are a food processor, they will have to learn
how to sell the improved profits resulting from solving a
retailer's problems through stocking your products
rather than the virtues of the products themselves.

And if you are a stockbroker, a banker, or an in-
surer, your representatives will have to learn how to sell
the improved profits resulting from solving a customer's
estate-planning problems through stocks and bonds,
certificates of deposit, or life insurance rather than the
particular attributes of any of these specific products themselves.

Planning Individual Account Penetration

Your decision to concentrate on top-tier penetration
requires one more area of sales management expertise.
This is a planning function. You must penetrate every
key account to its maximum contribution. You must
penetrate as quickly as possible because time is money,
both for you and for your customer. You must penetrate
at high levels to insure top-tier representation. You must

penetrate on a sequential basis so you will always be at work improving a key account's profit and avoid down time in applying your talent resources.

There is more. You must penetrate in such a way that you can upgrade your penetrations over time and migrate from them into new opportunities. You must penetrate the most significant customer problems on a priority timetable. In this way, the customer's most compelling needs are benefited first. Furthermore, you will be able to close off invasion routes for your competitors, who will be attracted to any gaps you leave unfilled.

You must accomplish these tasks with every key customer account because it is a miniature market of its own—a microcosm of an industry to which you are committed because you can help it improve its profits and it can help you improve your own.

Each account penetration plan that your representatives prepare is a business plan, a blueprint of how the profit contribution of a customer will be obtained. It is objectives-oriented. Its strategies are composed of the proposals that the representatives and their APACHE proposal partner have prepared for presentation. Their cumulative profit improvement adds up to the "product line" you will deliver to the account this year. It tells you how important you are to the customer.

In turn, the improved profit that will accrue to you is your customer's contribution. It tells you how important the customer is to you—how "key" its key account status really is. If your contribution to the customer turns out not to be significant, you will lose your position as a consultant. If the customer's contribution to you is not significant and cannot be made so, you should by the same token demote the customer to a vendor relationship.

Partnering in Profit

There is only one platform from which you can operate when your objective is to manage your key account penetration for improved profit on sales: that is to recognize the primacy of improved profit within your key account businesses and make it your No. 1 objective. Of all the dependencies on which key account penetration rests, first and foremost is the creation of a partnership in improved profit making with each customer.

Partnering in mutual profit improvement is the basis for win-win relationships. It requires a dedication to do your up-front homework, to get the facts and quantify their implications in dollar terms. It requires a dedication to install solutions rather than merely sell them. It requires a dedication to put them in place, monitor their contribution, and teach customer people how to maintain the contribution at the profit-improving rate you have proposed.

The dedications imposed by a commitment to partner in profit with your key accounts surround selling. At the front end is the requirement to study someone else's business. At the back end are the monitoring, measuring, and teaching requirements that must be carried on with someone else's people. This description may make partnering sound linear, like vendor selling. It is not. Partnering is an endless cycle where homework leads to a proposal, which leads to a sale, which leads to the afterwork following a sale, which leads to upgrading the sale and developing new information about the customer's business, which serves as homework for the next proposal—and so on, endlessly.

Partnering takes place at every stage of the process, because every stage involves the customer's people. The two most productive stages are the discovery of problems that can be solved together and the achievement of their solutions. This tells us the secret of key account partnerships. They are based on two kinds of rewards. One is learning: finding out how to solve a problem that is inhibiting a customer's profits. The other is achievement: proving that a solution works by delivering tangible results to the customer in the form of bankable dollars.

2

High-Margin Selling

How to Activate Top Customer Managers

High-margin selling to key account decision makers is a business of its own. It requires consultative sales strategy whose skills are mostly at a 180-degree variance from vendor skills. It requires sales representatives who are recruited according to consultant characteristics, and who are differently supported, differently compensated, and differently managed. They do not "yes . . . but" their way to overcome customer objections, they do not trial close, and they do not sell price performance, because they do not sell products.

In order to penetrate their accounts at high customer management levels where high margins are obtainable, key customer sales representatives must be trained in the consultative selling skills: the agenda for what takes place when the key account representative stands before the customer tier at the top. This is no-man's-land for the so-called professional sales representative. To sell at this level, only "the product of your product" can be sold—that is, only the improved profit it can deliver. How well this has been learned is revealed by how long it takes a key account representative to complete the five-step consultative selling cycle.

These are the two prime duties of your key account representatives: to become proficient in the consultative selling skills and to learn how to turn over the consultative selling cycle in the most rapid manner.

The sales management level is the most vital support source for key account representatives. It is true that they can sell without the three contributions that sales management should make to them. But you will pay the price. The best of your current force will leave and go elsewhere to a more conducive, more fully committed environment. The best of your candidates will prefer to sign on elsewhere. They have learned what to ask for up front. The rest will probably stay. That is where you will pay the price.

What do you need to provide as support? You must stake out a corporate position as the educator of your key customer industries on how they can improve profits, cost reduction, and productivity in the areas of their businesses that you affect. You must reach out and fertilize your total marketing strategy with the consultative selling platform of key account penetration. Further, you must indoctrinate the nonselling functions in your company as well.

This triple-barreled approach will maximize the value of the training you provide in the consultative selling skills. It will apply your company's resources against the customers who are its main sources of earnings. It will help safeguard your key account businesses from competition. And last but not least, it will give you the single best selling edge in your industry: It will define your business in relation to the central needs of your key customers, the needs they have to increase their profits.

Standing Before the Tier at the Top

Top-tier customer management deals rarely with vendors and then only under duress. They speak different languages. Vendors speak price and performance benefits. Management speaks value and profit contribution. Vendors speak costs. Management speaks return on investment. Vendors speak of their competitors. Management is concerned about its own. Vendors wonder when management will ever buy. Management wonders when vendor presentations will ever end.

Vendors who stand before their customer tier at the top will not do so for long or soon again. For consultative sellers to make a stand, and make it again and again, they must be prepared to speak the language of management, address its concerns instead of their own, and put to work their knowledge of the customer's business so that a demonstrable improvement—not just a shipment of goods—takes place.

Figure 1 shows the composition of the top management tier and the decision-making criteria it reacts to at its top and upper middle levels. In contrast, the criteria of the purchasing tier are markedly different.

Key account sales representatives who want to penetrate the top customer tier must position themselves to discuss, document, and deliver their answers to the question "How much profit will you add?" For them, that is their sales mission in a nutshell. It is what being a consultative sales representative is all about. A mix of three consultative skills is required for them to take the consultative position. One is the skill of knowing the customer's business well enough to know how a profit is made in that particular business and how it can be improved. A second skill is demonstrating an improvement.

The third skill is creating the close, continuing partnerships on the top tier that foster ongoing knowledge of the customer's business and the availability of top-tier managers to receive the sales representatives' proposals.

The key account representatives who stand before customer management in the role of their consultants assume a hybrid stance. They are not vending. They cannot be positioned as traditional sellers. Nor are they managing their customer's business. They cannot be positioned as peers. Above the one, they are below the other. Their closest analog is among the customer's own staff, not with anyone else from the outside. Internal

Figure 1.   Top-tier decision-maker criteria.

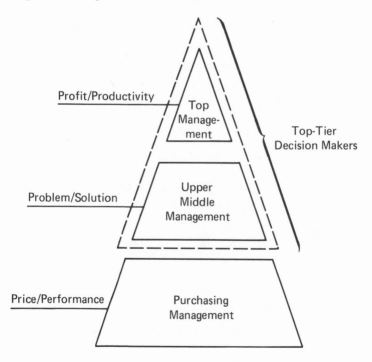

people who report to the top tier, who bring financially quantified solutions to it for proposal and disposal, and who must then implement them when they are budgeted provide the consultative sales representatives' most approximate role models.

Internal managers most often approach their top tier as the principals in a four-act play. Key account sales representatives should follow this scenario closely, both in sequence and in content.

ACT 1: "WHY DO YOU WANT TO SEE ME?"

Everyone who approaches top-tier management must offer justification. Management's brainpower is every company's most precious internal resource. It must be profitably engaged every minute. Downtime is time lost forever. Management knows what is profitable. Do you? it asks. Management knows what needs improvement to become more profitable. Do you? it asks.

Your sales representatives must be prepared to declare what they want to see their customer decision makers about. It must be a problem of significant concern. Or it must be a major opportunity. It must be current, significant, and be the kind of situation that appears solvable within a reasonable amount of time. Issues that meet these criteria are top-tier management's proper business. Any other issues—specifically those within the sales representatives' business—will bring the response that management is too busy with its own business to deal with them. Act 1 can be the final act unless the customer's business is spotlighted on center stage.

ACT 2: "WHAT DO YOU WANT ME TO DO ABOUT IT?"

Management-level decision makers make decisions. They do not contemplate idly. When you raise an issue with management, you cannot provoke intellectual curiosity without offering a remedy. Once management knows why you want its attention and agrees on the merit of your response, it next must know what you want it to do. It is your sales representatives who will, of course, end up doing something about the issues they have raised. But customer management must do something first: It must appropriate assets in the form of dollars and people.

Assets are allocated for solutions, either solutions that prevent problems or those that can relieve them in whole or in part. Management must be told what solutions are available to it. Some may already have been tried and failed. Should any of them be considered anew? Some attempts at solution may already be in implementation. Can they be reinforced? Should they be superseded before they fail or prove cost-ineffective? Is there a best solution—if so, how can we tell it is best? What can its contribution be expected to amount to?

When customer management evaluates solutions, it is not evaluating products, services, or systems. It may know little about them and care less. Top management assesses only the financial results of a solution, not its components or their performance. Operating managers will be more interested in both. But at the top, the dialog of act 2 will be principally in the dollar terms of how much profit you are prepared to offer management and how much, in return, you want as your reward.

ACT 3: "HOW DO I KNOW IT WILL WORK?"

If management likes what you want it to do—in other words, if it likes the amount of added profit you want it to be able to make—it will want to know how it can realize your proposal. How do I know the profits you promise will actually accrue? That is what top management means by "will it work?" It is not a question of whether the gears will mesh or the system will integrate—these will have to be demonstrated to operating management. At the top tier, a proposal works when it produces the profit output claimed for it. If it operates mechanically, chemically, or electronically but the profits are not forthcoming, it does not work.

Act 3 is where your key sales representatives must attest to the workability of their solution. They must document the profits, showing their source, their flow, and their cumulative total. They must also attest to the overall composition of their solution. In general, what major product components will it contain? What services? What does the system as a whole look like? How does it conform to state-of-the-art technology, and what is its track record? The specifics of its features and benefits will be relegated to the probings of operating management "downstairs."

Act 3 can therefore be divided into two sequential scenes. First, operating managers should be partnered with on the performance contributions of your proposals. Then, when a concensus agreement has been reached with them, the financial contributions should be proposed to top management. This phasing of approval permits top management to obtain the immediate concurrence of its operating decision makers: "Is this what you want? Will it work the way they say it will?" It also prevents incurring resentment at the operating levels from having a decision handed down instead of participating in handing it up.

ACT 4: "WHEN DO WE GET THE SHOW ON THE ROAD?"

When your key account sales representatives sell consultatively, the call to action will most likely come from the customer in act 4. As soon as your solution is perceived to work financially and operationally, top management will want to implement it. Time is money. Every minute's delay deprives them of promised profits.

Implementation consists of four elements. The first three concern what will be installed, when it will become operational, and who from each side will be involved. The fourth element is the sum total of the first three. What resources will have to be provided from the customer's business to match the resources contributed by your key account representative and his or her support services? Only when people—their time and talent—and money are allocated does something get done in business. You must be prepared to specify what both of you will have to put up in order to get the show on the road.

Your key account representatives must be trained to produce their four-act plays at a fast clip, requiring a minimum of props, and moving smoothly from one act to the next. Like all good plays, consultative proposals should be presented orally, leaving behind a copy of the libretto for each member of the audience. An hour, allowing time for interruptions, is the maximum length any performance should require. The audience has other plays to go to. As for your own people, they earn their pay only when they implement—not when they propose.

Where are the trapdoors under top management's carpet? They are everywhere. Act 1 can close out your performance if you focus on a problem that customer management does not perceive as significant or if you fail to describe a truly significant problem correctly in management terms. You will be dismissed as not understanding the customer's business.

If the solution you propose in act 2 pays out too little profit or is too late in coming, it may be rejected. If it is too great in amount, your credibility may be suspect. Can you really do what you say you can do? If you are deemed not credible, you will not be trusted with management's approval. Even worse, if your solution appears to be unlikely and you provide supportive testimony from another industry, although closely allied, or another company in your customer's industry, you may be summarily dismissed as not understanding the differences between your customer's business and all others.

In the event that fault is found with your financial documentation of profit contribution in act 3, especially if the errors are in your favor, your image or your credibility will be downgraded. You may nonetheless survive if the corrected contribution remains significant. If your profit analysis fails utterly, you will be dismissed as not understanding the first thing about the business of consultation in profit improvement.

Act 4 is the proof of the pudding. If you cannot implement, you will be dismissed as not understanding the second thing about the business of how to bring profits down to a customer's bottom line.

Five-Stepping the Consultative Selling Cycle

A key account sales representative going through the consultative selling cycle will take five steps. They are all forms of learning and teaching. The cycle contains two types of elements. Planning the account's penetration and generating the proposal are the least time-consuming elements. But the other three elements are dependent on customer people: their cooperation, their information, and their instigation of acceptance inside the customer's organization structure. When the selling cycle turns over slowly, people problems are probably the reason. This puts a premium on the ability of key account representatives to achieve multiple partnerships with operating, financial, and managerial levels in their accounts.

The five-step selling cycle starts with data basing and proceeds to penetration planning, preliminary partnering, proposing, and implementing. As logic suggests, they are generally sequential. Frequently, however, data basing must be returned to, planning must be revised, and the initial partnerings must be reinstituted with different influencers or decision makers. In these instances, the cycle is less of a progressive curve than a zigzag.

1. *Data basing.* Knowledge of the customer's business is the basis for penetration planning, partnering, and proposing. Two things can usually be said about it. Unlike product knowledge, you probably do not have customer knowledge at the start. And, again unlike product knowledge, you probably cannot acquire the customer knowledge you need, or validate the knowledge you have, without getting into the customer's business. From the very outset, partnering skills are crucial.

The vital components of your key customer data base are twofold. The first component is the customer's currently perceived critical problems and opportunities in the business functions you can affect. What are they, where are they, what are the dollar values the customer has put on them, and who are the decision makers who will determine what action, if any, is to be taken about them? The second component is the customer's current solutions. What are they, what are the dollar values attributed to them, where are they deficient, and who are their advocates?

When you have digested these two areas of information, you will be able to add a third component to your data base. What are your own solutions to the customer's problems and unachieved opportunities, and what are the incremental dollar values they can contribute when compared against the customer's current solutions? This component will allow your APACHE data system to be the proposal partner of your key account representatives.

2. *Penetration planning.* The data base predetermines each key account's penetration plan and the partnering and proposing that execute it. That is why key account selling is data-dependent. The plan deals with the data on an as-if basis: as if the data *is* the customer's business as far as your sales opportunity is concerned. It then asks and answers the following questions:

What is our optimal solution for each customer problem and opportunity? What is its dollar value to the customer? To us? What is it composed of—what products and services? Is it a superproduct, as discussed in Appendix 1? What priority rank order should we advocate for its presentation? Who are the decision makers involved? Taking all of our solutions together, what is the total contribution we can make to this customer? What is the customer's total expected contribution to us? What is our revenue-to-expense ratio to achieve it?

The penetration plan is your operating manual with each account. It should serve two purposes. It will allow you to manage the account's penetration, determining how much of its potential contribution you are reaching, whether or not you are on schedule, and what unexploited opportunities remain for proposing. This is the plan's internal function. It should have an external use as well. It should be positioned by your key account representatives as the mutual plan of their partnerships with customers. Each representative should prepare the plan with customer participation, making sure that its priorities and assumptions are those of the account. The representative should be equally certain that customer decision makers understand how much profit im-

provement he or she expects to bring them and what
their own commitment of resources will have to be if
they want it.

    3. *Preliminary partnering.* Partnering begins when
your key account representatives share their penetration
plans with customer decision makers and influencers.
From there, it must go on to include a broad spectrum of
top-tier customer managers: division and department
managers; financial administrators; functional managers
in sales, engineering, and manufacturing; and operating
managers.

    With each category of management, mutual objec-
tives must be established and agreements reached on the
most acceptable strategic approach to achieve them. Information must be encouraged to flow both ways so that
everybody contributes something to your customer data
base and everybody takes something away, only to return it in more accurate, fact-enriched form.

    Partners will emerge in several guises. Information
partners will show and tell but do nothing. Action partners will work with your representatives but will not necessarily go to bat for them. Contrariwise, advocate-type
partners will speak for your representatives at high customer levels but will play no active role in getting the
work done. Somewhere along the line, your sales representatives will have to identify their mentor partners,
who will guide them through the customer's political and
social systems, steering them to supporters and away
from delayers or apparent nay-sayers.

    Partnering at many different position levels with
many different personalities, professional cultures, and
political relationships is a complex task. It is the consultative sales representatives' master skill. Unless they can
identify their mission with each potential partner's own
objectives and create a participative strategy that takes

those objectives into consideration, they will essentially be reduced to vending, no matter what other skills they may possess.

4. *Proposing.* Each proposal to improve a key account's profit or productivity or operating performance should be one of the modules in the account's penetration plan. It should bear a priority ranking and, whenever possible, flow out of a previous proposal and into a following one. The knowledge of what to propose, to whom it should be proposed, and when the proposal should be made must come out of customer partnering.

Your APACHE data system is your sales representatives' proposal partner. In communion with it, each representative can call up the optimal solution to the customer problems and opportunities contained in the APACHE data. The representatives do this by asking their proposal partner to suggest a survey of solutions, some that may have been proposed previously to solve similar problems and others that APACHE will retrieve from its knowledge bank. They can also mix and match the piece parts of two or more solutions, playing the "What if . . . ?" game with them: What if we add this from here and subtract that from there: How does it affect our ability to improve the customer's profit?

If there are optional solutions, each should be worked up by the sales representatives and their APACHE proposal partner so they can be discussed with their customer partners. Even if there is only one clear-cut solution, it should be preproposed to their customer partners so that their inputs, and their support, can be obtained. When the proposal is actually presented, there must be no surprises among your sales representatives or their customer partners.

Each proposal should be looked on as serving three purposes. The first purpose, of course, is to sell at a high-margin price that is commensurate with the customer's improved profit. Second, a proposal should prepare the way for its follow-on proposals. Third, successful proposals should be recycled into the APACHE data system so that they can be used over and over again as references for proposals yet to come.

5. *Implementing.* Proposals are born in data and mature profitably or perish in implementation. No matter how optimal your solution may be, it is valueless if its integration into the customer's business falls short of enabling it to make the full contribution of profit you have proposed.

Implementation is the acid test of your ability to convert promise into performance. It is your center court opportunity to cement partnerships, earn your way into further learning about the customer's business, and be first in line to propose your next strategy to improve customer profit.

No matter what business you are in, and no matter what specific aspects of integrating your solutions you must observe, there are three common denominators of implementation to which you must adhere.

As quickly as possible, you must install your solution in the customer's operations. It must start to function. It must begin to produce the profit stream you have proposed. The onset of profit is the crucial element of implementation. Every day of delay—in many situations, every hour and every minute—has a dollar equivalent that subtracts from the promise of your proposal. Conversely, every day of incremental profit is a bonus.

Monitoring your solution, not just its function performance but also its delivery of improved profit, must go hand in glove with your installation. Your sales representatives and their customer partners will have to agree beforehand on the criteria for monitoring—exactly what is expected—and the milestones when it is due. A monitoring system and periodic joint progress meetings are

necessary requirements to insure common perceptions of
what is being achieved.

Finally, there can be no implementation without
training the customer's people in how to operate the solution, maintain it, and measure the solution's contribution. Training helps insure the achievement of your
proposal. It spares your customer an added cost, thereby
increasing profit. Similarly, it also spares you the added
cost of providing endless service, repairs, and warran-
teed replacement parts due to customer ineptitude that
can seriously injure your own profit on sales.

The beginning point of every consultative selling cycle is clear: It is always data-based. But when does a
cycle end? It is tempting to say that the customer acceptance of your proposal is the natural end point. But getting the customer's improved profits to flow during
implementation is really the signal that your original
promise is on the way to realization and that you have
earned the right to propose once again, initiating a new
cycle as the next stage of an endless process of profit
improvement.

Preempting the Industry Educator Position

A top-tier sales organization is a mighty information
machine. Because it is industry-based, it learns a lot
about each key industry it serves—industry economics,
key financial ratios, performance averages and norms,
market trends and projections. It is customer-intensive
as well, so it learns a great deal about each key account—
financial ratios, performance averages and norms compared to industry criteria, trends, projections, and an
account's customer markets.

There are two constituencies for this wealth of information, in the form of either raw data or reports to which

you have added some value by custom-tailored process-ing. For industry data, the industries themselves present you with a potential market. So do companies that may be searching out growth opportunities outside their own industries. For customer data, you may have two mar-kets: the customers themselves, for whom their own in-formation will be the basis for proposals to improve their profit; and your customer's own key account representa-tives.

The raw materials stockpiling, manufacture, and dis-tribution of this information, both for internal and exter-nal consumption, offers a correlate to the stockpiling, manufacture, and distribution of your products. It en-ables you to take a position as the preeminent source of industry information supply.

In order to dominate an industry's perception of you as knowledgeable in its business, there is no substitute for being its preemptive educator. Consultative selling is knowledge-based selling. To sell from knowledge, there are two requisites. You must have the data. You must also have the repute for having the data. If you meet the requisites, you provide your sales force with the benefit of selling from an acknowledged industry-smart corpo-rate platform.

The answer to the question "What is the best image for a top-tier sales strategy?" is to be recognized as the leading industry educator in each key industry you want to penetrate. There are three approaches to accomplish-ing this objective.

The institute approach. Your industry data base can become the reactor core of a business unit called an insti-tute: the Institute of Productivity Improvement if you sell office product systems, the Institute of Risk Manage-ment if you sell fire-protection systems, the Institute of Critical Care Therapeutics if you sell hospital equipment. The institute can be set up as a quasi-independent but

wholly owned subsidiary. It should distribute its information free from overt sales contamination through multiple media such as books, magazines, newsletters,
videofilms and discs, seminars and conferences, and
traveling road shows. Customers and prospects alike are
its audience. If your business is involved with a public
service such as environment or energy, this can be
featured. The involvement of your products is legitimate
wherever they fit the message.

The corporation-as-educator approach. With or
without an institute, the corporation itself can benefit the
key account sales thrust by dedicating its overall position
to educating its markets. The corporate theme should
emphasize this dedication. So should the architectural
layout of corporate headquarters. The main entrance
can, for example, show the optimal use of corporate
products at a customer location under actual conditions,
supplemented by photographs and continuous films. The
annual report and executive meetings with investment
analysts, advertising of both the product and institutional
types, and publicity can all be used to propagate the
educator position. You and your key account representatives should author articles for customer industry media,
speak at its conventions, and demonstrate your educational contributions at its trade shows and exhibits.

The sales force-as-learners/teachers approach.
Consultative sales representatives are teachers of profit
improvement to top-tier customer decision makers. If
they teach well, they will sell well. To teach well, they
must be taught well. A key account sales organization
must therefore be a year-round educational organization
whose curriculum is customer profit improvement based
on the consultative selling skills.

All new key account sales representatives should be
trained in consultative skills. This is ingrade training. All
practicing key account representatives should be periodi-

cally retrained in the skills that enable them to be properly positioned, to prepare profit improvement proposals, and to be good business partners with their customers. This is upgrade training. The same kind of training should be given to regional sales managers and national account managers. Outside the sales force, consultative selling skills should be communicated to product development people, financial people, managers of marketing functions, and your own top management— your own top tier—so they will know how to support your key account sales operations.

This three-pronged approach says many things to its constituents. To current and prospective key account customers, it underscores your enduring interest in their industry and validates your capability base for providing them with substantive help. To your key account sales force, it proves your long-term commitment to support consultative selling strategies with their high-level customers. To potential new hires, it fortifies their belief that you offer a competitively superior career path. And to your own upper levels of management, it helps them position their business, allocate proper funds to support your key account plans, and take on some consultative characteristics themselves when they sell to upper-level customers in their stratospheric contacts.

Fertilizing the Total Marketing Strategy

In most companies, selling is regarded as a subservient marketing function. Others hedge, marrying sales and marketing in a single function. Marketing is the creation of customer perceptions of premium value for a business. Since high-margin prices are the reward for perceived premium value, marketing strategy obviously has the ability to make a serious positive or negative impact on consultative selling to key accounts. Total marketing strategy must be made supportive to key customer penetration.

Marketing itself, as an amalgam of functions, should be a top-tier process. Unlike the sales function, marketing has no bottom-tier constituency. Perceptions of premium value need to be created only among the market segments—the key industries—where consultative selling will take place. No one else needs to be marketed to, since lower-tier segments—industries that are not key because they are not among the 20 percent or so that provide up to 80 percent of profitable sales volume—will not be asked to pay premium prices for vended values.

Once marketing is seen as a top-tier function, urgency for close correlation of its component functions with top-tier selling will become apparent.

The key account selling data base is industry-dedicated and customer-oriented. It can therefore easily become the marketing data base as well, since the same industries and the same companies will be marketed to. Marketing, among all the corporate functions, must be market-driven. Unfortunately, it is not always so, tending to be driven separately by one or another of its component functions that may be in organizational favor at any given time.

Marketing's prime standard of performance must be to support key account sales penetration. If it cannot do this, it can do nothing. The marketing plan should have the objective of providing optimal support to achieve the combined objectives of all the individual key account penetration plans and to deliver this support in the most cost-effective manner. The standard of performance for marketing cost-effectiveness is achieved when upward revisions in marketing allocations would not proportionately increase key account profit contribution to you;

conversely, downward revisions would decrease your key account profits in a disproportionate ratio.

This perspective of marketing harnesses it to sales, exactly the opposite of traditional policy in companies that practice vendor sales to both top and bottom tiers throughout the industries they serve. In a two-tier organization, marketing should be meshed with the top-tier sales function once it has become key market-, key account-driven. Every function in the company, the non-selling functions as well as marketing, should be supportive to top-tier selling, since they all depend on its revenues for their sustenance.

As key account penetration becomes increasingly important to business growth strategy in the new 1980-2000 generation, two-tier selling and, along with it, top-tier concentration will become the fundamental sales strategy. Fallout strategies from it will affect the marketing function, most notably in the present universalist concept of its mission. There will be less and less mass marketing, since mass markets will continue their present fractionalization into more and more finite segments. Along with the shortage of mass markets will be vast reductions in full product lines that offer something for everybody. Production, marketing, and sales will stringently focus on the big winners in every line and let the others slide. Marketing will then be able to cease its attempt to keep every product and market manager happy by supporting full lines and stroking every customer industry in the corporate portfolio.

There are five components of total marketing strategy that must be fertilized: That is, they must be correlated with key account sales penetration strategy. Marketing will have to concentrate on key industries, key customer accounts within each key industry and the big winner products, services, and systems sold to them.

It will have to support the key account penetration selling strategies in each industry, using the same sales style
of customer profit improvement and the same sales content that offers documentation. In every instance, the
crunch criterion will have to be: "Does what we are doing support the key account sales representatives—does
it help them shorten the consultative selling cycle by
being able to stand before top-tier customer decision
makers and make more and more sizable high-margin
sales?"

1. *Advertising and sales promotion.* Two-tier sales
strategy requires two-tier advertising strategy. Lower-
tier sales and advertising should both vend. Advertisements and sales promotion brochures, catalogs, and
product announcements directed to purchasing agents
and engineering-acculturated functional managers such
as data processing managers, telecommunications managers, risk managers, equipment standardization com-
mittee managers, and the like should be price-
performance advertisements. Features and benefits
should prevail over claims of profit improvement except
in the case of markets where the purchasing-type functions are being educated to demand profit, cost, or productivity benefits along with performance results.

Advertising and collateral sales support materials
designed for top customer tier audiences will have to be
completely different. They will have to be profit-themed.
Products and systems may not ever be shown. You
should not proclaim your own ability to improve customer profits, nor should your key account "experts" or
their support staffs be starred as the instigators of better
bottom lines. Instead, your top-tier advertising should
showcase your key customers. Profit improvement
claims should be their claims, testimony their testimony,

results their results. They should have high appetite value to make your other key customers and prospects hunger for similar infusions of new profits.

Consultative selling advertises itself by the case method. It serves many purposes. It documents your profit improvement capability. It promotes your track record. It professionalizes your consultative approach, freeing you from the need to blow your own horn. And at the same time, it stimulates your customers to ask their key account representatives the opening question, "Can you do the same thing for us?"

2. *Product nomenclature.* For the vendor market, it probably makes little if any difference what a product or system is named. So tangential is the usual impression that most vended products are unnamed. They bear only serial numbers or letters, like the 4600 or the Series J. If they have names, they most likely describe what the product is, such as a New Dimension, instead of what it does that can help improve customer profit, such as the APACHE Proposal Partner Data System.

In top-tier selling, product or process names can have an additive effect on key account penetration if they are correlated with improved customer profit. Big winner products should be named with their eventual destination in mind as a component in a profit-improvement system. The same reasoning applies to names for product-related services for maintenance, upgrading, the resupply of consumables, and leasing. What do their names say about their contribution to the system's mission— what synergy does their nomenclature add to the system as a whole?

If the same product is to be marketed to top-tier industries and vended to the bottom tier, no problem is created. It can be named for its top-tier mission and serialized for the other. It can also be painted in different colors for each tier of an industry, packaged differently, and otherwise distinguished.

3. *Trade shows and industry exhibits.* If advertising can be described as selling in print, your appearances at trade shows and industry exhibits represent selling by booth. What applies to advertising should apply here, too. Your booth theme should teach key customers about your profit-improvement capabilities. Advertised case histories can be bound for distribution and shown in continuous video formats. If your products lend themselves to participative demonstrations, you can permit prospective customers to prove their profit-improving effect for themselves in a hands-on manner.

Trade shows are widely used to collect alleged leads, generally composed of names and inquiries that are followed up in an inverse ratio to their number. It is probably just as well, because the 80-20 rule suggests that the bulk of them will result in either no sale or only marginally profitable sales. If you are seeking vending leads, they may be justifiable. But if you want to position your appearance to reinforce key account sales, you will want to find ways to zero in on key customers as distinct from—and perhaps even to the exclusion of—low-margin tier representatives.

What you say about yourself as a profit improver, what you show and teach about your abiities and their results, along with the consultative manner in which you communicate your mission, will be self-selecting. It can either bring you a new record number of unconvertible names or a few new key customers who are highly convertible at high margins.

4. *Annual report.* The 10-K is a legal document. Its market is the SEC and the investment community. The annual report is a marketing document. Among its other

intended audiences, your key customers look to it for restatement of your commitment to them, for additional case materials and news about the strengthening of your capabilities, your continuing education program in consultative selling, fertilization of your nonselling functions with profit-improvement knowledge and motivation—to learn, in short, how seriously you take your consultative position. Security analysts do the same.

Most annual reports are product catalogs. Some show the factory. Among the worst are reports that attempt to humanize their companies: "All we are is people," they say, and that is what they display. Products, processes, plants, and people all ignore the source of the funds that pay for them, the top-tier industries they serve.

Every year's annual report should be a report card to key accounts on how you have helped them improve their profits again last year as the best way of adding to the values of your shareholders and theirs as well. Within that context, your people, products, and plants can take on properly contributory meanings.

5. *Executive spokesmen.* Your own top-tier executives can be carriers of your profit-improvement mission statement in their appearances before key industry groups and in one-to-one sessions with their peers in your key customer companies. On the other hand, they can deposition you in one fell swoop. Their conversion is the final link in the chain of marketing strategies to support key account penetration.

Today's board chairmen, presidents, and other top-level managers still tend to come from a corporate culture where big was best; where market share and volume bespoke success; and where breadth, diversity, and mass were the magic words. You must help educate them in the dynamics of key account selling based on a consultative approach to top-tier decision makers. If you succeed, they can be the most powerful converts to your side. They also have the ears of other powerful decision makers in your key customer companies who, as influencers, can shorten the cycle for your key account sales representatives when they come before them.

These five challenges to fertilize your total marketing strategy represent the hardest sell of all—selling the doctrine of key account penetration internally. It is a classic example of top-tier selling. As such, it will provide an excellent test of your consultative selling skills.

Indoctrinating the Nonselling Functions

Companies that are the ablest penetrators of their key customers make consultative selling a corporate policy, not just a sales strategy. They convert their entire organizations into improvers of customer profit, starting with the sales and marketing functions that lay hands on their key accounts and working inwards to the nonselling functions. They make everyone customer sensitive, customer responsive, and customer serving.

A unified front gives key account representatives total corporate support over and above functional sales and marketing support. It gives the customer a concerted set of attitudes and behavior patterns to deal with. The pressure the customer feels to improve profits is consistent. Everyone carries the same message. Each time they do business with the customer, they want to leave improved profits behind.

Three nonselling functions are the most essential for you to bring over to the consultative way: research and development, product or service engineering, and finance.

1. *Research and development.* Key account pene-

tration strategy reaches its zenith when it permeates the laboratory. Instead of building products and process that offer scientific challenge—that are built because they can be built better than anyone else can build them—penetration strategy gets to steer development in the direction of offering maximum profit improvement to your top-tier markets. Customer approval rather than the envy or admiration of competitive scientists becomes the foremost R&D objective.

Research must be taught to make what can be sold consultatively; that is, what can be sold at high margins because of its superior ability to improve customer profit. This requires R&D to be a consumer of market fact and a heavy user of the key account data system's knowledge banks on customer problems and opportunities. Customer knowledge, not technical capability, must be their starting point when they allocate dollars for development. Their payoff will not come just because they make something better. It will occur only when they have made it better able to improve customer profitability. Otherwise, it will have little or no value in key account selling.

The initial inquiries that go into technical research and development must be market research. This gives technical people their direction. It brings the market in to them before they invest their fast-fleeting time and talent and in advance of their emotional involvement with a specific method or outcome.

2. *Product engineering*. Most products are overengineered. In other words, they are overcosted so that they are overly difficult to sell at high margins or in a manner that can improve customer profit. This is not an argument against quality engineering. It is, instead, an appeal to permit your key customers to influence the type and amount of quality they need by specifying the profit contribution they expect.

Products have two objectives: They must meet minimal performance standards, and they must meet maximum profit-improvement standards. The task of product engineering is to determine how to satisfy performance requirements while at the same time deliver superior profit-improvement capability. Exceeding or falling below minimum performance that can maximize profit contribution is unacceptable management of product development.

Customer standards for improved profit and product engineering standards are often far apart. As with R&D, the customer's standards must be brought into the product engineering process. When "the quality goes in," product development engineers should be able to role play the key account sales representative standing before a top-tier decision maker. What words are the product engineers enabling the sales representative to say? What dollar values are they enabling him or her to sell? What product-performance benefits are required to help deliver those values? By the answers to these questions, the engineers will know what to build and why.

3. *Finance*. Consultative selling is value-based selling. Price is a function of the value of new profits that are brought down to the customer's bottom line. Since value will always differ from customer to customer and from project to project, there can be no standard price list for the product and service systems sold to top-tier customers. The sole generalization that can be made about key account pricing is that it is set to achieve high margins.

Lack of standardization is the bugaboo of your corporate controller and vice-president of finance. The world they live in is concerned with improving your own company's profits. Their awareness must be heightened to understand the dependent nature of their mission on your mission to improve customer profits. Along with your key account representatives, your costing and pricing people should be taught the consultative selling skills and taken into the consultative proposal process, where customer profit improvement is quantified. They can help the quantification procedure. They can also learn how to help your sales force when necessary, either internally or as a member of the sales support team accompanying key account representatives in their customer penetration.

Mobilizing the nonselling functions of R&D, product engineering, and finance on behalf of key account penetration is a tough but necessary task. None of these people are sales people. Many of them abhor sales for its extraversion and extreme people orientation. For similar reasons, they may distrust or demean sales representatives. They believe that if they "invent it smart, make it good, and price it fair," anyone can sell it. For them, the customer is the last stop in the capital turnover process instead of the first. Science and finance are seen as the sources of profit, sales is the outlet valve, and customer needs are roadblocks in the way of pure science and low-cost marketing.

A key account sales force works with one hand behind its back in such an environment. Only when the people who make your products, cost them, and price them work cooperatively with your key account representatives can consultative selling be planned to bring its full power to bear on top-tier penetration.

3
Multilevel Alliance Structuring

How to Insure Customer Continuity

The process of key account selling begins at the narrow end of a funnel, where a single selling message of improved profit is inserted. It emerges through the wide end custom-tailored in several different ways to meet the specific needs of each type of customer manager in the top tier. This contrasts with vendor selling, which originates at the funnel's wide end. A diversity of price and performance specifications is then focused on a single purchase decision maker.

Vendors sell to a homogeneous target, the manager of a customer's purchasing function. At their level, the frame of reference for selling is competitive price and performance. At the multiple levels of the top tier, several frames of reference determine whether or not value is perceived and, if so, how much. Key account sales representatives must sell at each of these managerial levels. They must speak its unique language to deliver the same essential message, customizing it so that they can build a sale and, at the same time, structure an ongoing alliance at each level.

A key account representative's job can be defined in three ways: Bring back sales, bring back new customer information that can lead to sales, but leave behind alliances with top-tier decision makers.

Sometimes a sale will build an alliance. More often alliances help build sales. Because they are diverse, they challenge representatives to develop a broad understanding of their customer's business organization. Because alliances are highly functional, with each level devoted to its own microcosm of the corporate universe, representatives must develop a narrow specialization in several customer business operations. These are additional ways of defining what it means to say that every key account representative must "know the customer's business." There is no way they can achieve this objective without allying themselves with the customer managers who perform the crucial functions of the business into which the representatives sell.

There are four levels on which alliances must be structured in a key customer account. Three of them are in the upper management tier. The fourth is the familiar purchasing level, where the traditional adversary relationship now calls for conversion into a more partnerable affiliation.

Alliances with Top Management

By selling as a consultant, a key account representative obtains access up and down the entire vertical chain of a customer's organization. This includes the topmost level of chief operating officer, usually the president. If you sell to a minor division or subsidiary of a large customer company, your top ally may be its president. Selling to several divisions, a major division, or to the corporate management level itself will require you to partner at the top at the company level as well as at divisional levels.

Customer presidents will join in alliances with key account representatives if, but only if, their self-interest is engaged. At their level, there are three principal interests:

1. *Financial improvement.* Chief operating officers are mainly preoccupied with the bottom line—profits. They view their businesses as money machines. For the most part of their daily routine, they are on the lookout for as many ways as possible to convert investments into superior return. If you can position yourself with them in this context, they can include your representatives among their investment options.

Presidents focus on returns. The accountability they have to their various constituencies demands it. Employees, shareholders, directors, and security analysts all lean on them to produce increased profits. Their stake in the presidents, and the presidents' stake in them, put constant pressure on generating improved profitability. In selling to presidents in a consultative manner, you can help relieve some of this pressure. You are representing an added chance to earn new profits if they will ally with you.

2. *People improvement.* Although presidents are fixated on returns, they must never lose sight of where returns come from. Profits are made by their people. They are the presidents' prime capital resource. If you can help improve the knowledge, competence, and productivity of strategically placed people, you can ally yourself as a partner in one of the presidents' own major missions.

What can their people learn from you? You can improve their ability to reduce the costs of their operations so that they will become less of a drain on internal funds, require a lower investment, or be able to return higher profit even from the original investment. You can also improve their ability to enhance sales revenues. If their abilities are upgraded in these vital areas, their profit contributions can be increased and their productivity stepped up by the amount they add to revenues for each dollar of investment in them.

3. *Operational improvement.* All customer operations are cost centers. By their nature, only a few can ever become profit centers. If you can bring down a cost center's investment base by streamlining its operations, consolidating functions, eliminating steps in its processes, or reducing its need for labor, energy, or materials, you can create a natural commonality of interest with customer presidents.

Presidents often ask themselves—and they are often asked by others—"How competitive are we?" By this, they mean many things: How good is our product, our people, and our promotion? They also run an ongoing audit of their operations to determine how competitive they are. They call it cost efficiency. It provides a useful index of just how efficiently their operations are converting a dollar of investment into a dollar of sales or productivity. When you help presidents improve their cost efficiency, you are assisting them in making their own businesses more competitive; that is, you are joining with them to help them maintain their market position, add to it, or regain it. These are always among the most paramount issues confronting decisions at the top tier.

Vendor sales representatives remain largely unaware of the interfaces that they may have in common with a customer president. Even if they have the awareness, they lack the ability to implement it so they can form alliances. They are often obsessed with a desire to "get upstairs." But it is the wrong obsession. The true objective is to be able to form a continuing alliance upstairs so that your representatives can go back again and again—indeed, so that their presence will be regarded as an ongoing added value by customer people at the top.

Because vendors are unable to translate into selling action the common denominators that exist between customer presidents and their suppliers, many of them regard a presidential alliance as a preposterous assumption. In reality, it has a recognizable basis in fact. People at a customer's top tier are immersed every day in selling situations. Everyone from top and middle management levels approaches them with something to sell: a new business venture or new product idea, an expansion of staff or facilities, or a new market penetration. They approach presidents and their committees in a consultative mode. They request the appropriations they seek on the basis of their ability to contribute a superior return.

This is the only way to approach the top, because it is the only way the top approaches investing its funds. When you sell as a consultant, you replicate the approach that is comfortable to customer top decision makers. Vendors, however, ask management to buy price/performance. Not only is management unskilled in making this type of commitment, it is also uncomfortable at being asked to play a purchasing role. Accordingly, it sends vendors back downstairs.

Alliances with Financial Management

Customer financial managers, either controllers or financial vice-presidents, share their presidents' criteria for evaluating the desirability of major purchases. They, too, are motivated by return on investment. Forming alliances at their level will require, for the most part, a similar strategy.

Financial managers regard themselves as keepers of the corporate checkbook. In that capacity, they are just as concerned as their top managers about what comes into their bank accounts. Even more than presidents, though, they focus on what goes out. They tend to be highly cost-conscious, auditing with exactitude the amounts of investment required to achieve a return as well as the size and nature of the return itself. As the focal points for the corporate struggle for funds, they more than anyone else are aware of the horns of the dilemma posed by any investment situation:

1. What if I make the investment? Will a better one come along tomorrow after I am out of funds?
2. What if I don't make the investment? Suppose a better one does not come along?

It is understandable that controllers are cautious. If they are approached with a vendor's characteristic persuasiveness, their inherent defenses will be heightened. They find a safe haven in numbers—the financial facts of a proposition to buy. Numbers are their words. They speak of reading them, letting the numbers tell them things, and getting their message. In order to partner with them, you will have to talk to them in their own language.

Financial managers are called money managers for good reason. Money is their unit of communication. For them, it talks. It converses with them in terms of its rate of return, its discounted cash flow, and its present value. Financial management is always in the market for money. They want to invest it, to put it to work for their businesses so that it will earn more money, which, in turn, will give them more money to invest, and so on.

They are the customer's investment managers. To form alliances with them, your representatives will have to provide them with new investment opportunities in the form of profit proposals.

Controllers and directors of customer financial functions never lack for places to put money to work in their businesses. What they do lack, however, is the funds themselves. If your business is going to have relevance for them as an ally, it will hardly ever be due to your products or services—unless they can be used in the financial function itself. Your relevance will depend on the new investment dollars you represent and how dependably they can be obtained.

Alliances with Functional Management

The managers of customer business functions are immersed in problems. These are the problems of supervising and administering their operations. They live in a world of people problems, productivity problems, manufacturing problems, quality control problems, inventory control problems, sales problems—whatever their function happens to be, it will have several of these problems as a normal consequence of its day-to-day activities. Business function managers want relief from their problems. They want their attendant costs removed. They want their opportunities expanded for greater sales revenues and productivity.

As a result, their principal concerns are to be knowledgeable in three areas:

1. *How to improve their operations*. What options exist for improvement, how they work to deliver improvement, and what mix of the options will provide the optimal results.

2. *When to improve their operations*. What timing is optimal for the introduction of improvements, how they can best be sequenced, and when the payoff on an improvement can be expected.
3. *Where to improve their operations*. What parts of their processes are the best starting points, how they can be improved most cost-effectively, and where an improvement can next be migrated so that its impact can be multiplied.

Based on these principal concerns, it is easy to understand why approaching functional managers by trying to sell them your product or service is unlikely to make a sale. Nowhere in their areas of concern is the concern for products. They care only for how products can affect their operations and when and where to implement them. Their functions are their context for judging what fits and what doesn't, what works and what won't, what is a good buy and what isn't.

The vendor sales approach that says "I want to sell you something" is meaningless when it is directed to a business function manager. It is, literally, out of context; that is, it has no perceived relation to his or her function. To say "I would like to work with you" is equally meaningless. The only approach that makes sense is to adopt the consultative approach and say "I can help improve your operation, both in performance and in profit." This addresses the business function manager's concept of a problem. It also addresses the function manager in his or her role of problem solver.

Alliances with Purchasing Management

The traditional interests of purchasing managers cannot be partnered with in consultative alliances. Competitive price-performance considerations are not the consultant's stock-in-trade. Instead, a new set of standards must be introduced into the purchasing relationship to upgrade its areas of concern to the same level as those held by business function managers. Value considerations must replace price. The financial aspects of performance must be substituted for physical, chemical, mechanical, hydraulic, or electronic performance results as buying criteria. Benefits must be recast in dollar terms from the traditional measurements of pounds, gallons, bytes, or man-days.

Alliances with purchasing management have two objectives. The first is to create a consultative partnership that will enable your representatives and their customer purchasers to develop profit improvement proposals in collaboration with each other. Then, together, they can take them upstairs for joint presentations at the top tier.

The second objective of a purchasing alliance is to develop an implementation exchange. As an outsider, your representatives can help their purchasers with access to information, access to higher-level management inside the purchasers' organization, and by educating them in the profit-improvement approach to evaluating proposals. Because the purchasers are insiders, they can help your representatives with internal data on customer needs, decision-making practices, and the politics of functional management relations. In these ways, the basis for an alliance exists.

Alliance Objectives

The objectives of all key account alliances are similar, regardless of the level at which they are to be achieved. Their overriding goal is to insure customer continuity. Unless your key account relationships are continuous, there will be no way for you to maximize the profit opportunity that a major customer represents. Unless you can keep your key customers, everything else is academic. You will be helped in this goal by following three strategies in your alliances: collaborate, educate, and negotiate.

Collaborate. In key account situations, it takes two to make every sale. Your representatives cannot sell alone. Their customer allies must help them sell within the customer's company. On each side, there must be the same dedication, the same commitment, and the same conviction that a sale will add genuine values to both parties. When a sale is finally made, it should be impossible to tell who really made it. This is the test of a true collaboration: The sale is the thing, not the seller.

Educate. Your organization and your key customers must do more with each other than buy and sell if your relationships are to be continuous. Along with making new dollars, you should both be making new information available to the people on each side who will be collaborating on proposing sales. Not only must you both earn as a result of your relationships. You must both learn as well. Professional growth and personal growth have to attend profit growth.

Negotiate. The main subject area of the mutual education between collaborators is how to improve profits. This requires continuing back-and-forth dialog. The flow of inputs must be unimpeded. Suggestions and recommendations will need to be aired. The environment that is ideal will be rich in options yet sparse in negative thinking, put-downs, editorializing, or defensiveness against anything that is "not invented here." Free-swinging relationships where there is a high degree of give-and-take allow you and your customers to avoid losing out on important peripheral and futuristic opportunities. They also allow you to cash in fully on solving the problems that are in the forefront of awareness.

These objectives are easier said than accomplished. They depend on your ability to create a significant transformation in how you relate to your key account decision makers and their influencers. The result of this transformation is called a partnership.

Partnership Requirements

Partners are not simply customer decision makers who approve your proposals. Partners are your representatives' coaches. They counsel your representatives on how to get things done inside their companies, vector them around obstacles, and define the players for them. Partners are your representatives' blockers. They run interference for them, dealing behind the scenes with objectors and foot-draggers. Partners are your representatives' anchors. They act as their alter egos, their main contact points within the customer companies. Partners are your representatives' version of "Deep Throat," their news analysts of what is really going on with the customer and what its probable implications are most likely to be.

Partners are your representatives' chief implementers. They are their introducers to top-tier customer managers. They influence other managers to be accepting of your people. They take the major risk of lending their auspices to you, sticking their necks out on your behalf, and putting themselves on the line as testifiers for your ability to improve their companies' profits. These invaluable attributes tell you why partners are indispensable to a consultative relationship. They also tell you why partners must be protected as well as cultivated. If you lose a partner, you may very well lose the entire account.

Maintaining partners imposes three requirements:

1. *You must participate.* You must be actively involved with your customers, working closely with them to learn how to help solve their business problems that you can affect. This means more than just proposing and selling. It means finding out when and where they like you to get involved with their problems and then getting into them at that point. It means investing up-front time to study their situations, laying down your fact base before proceeding into the selling cycle and building your acceptance within their organizations on a step-by-step basis.

2. *You must commit.* You must plan a long-term growth relationship with each key account, viewing it as an essential part of your business in the same way you regard guaranteeing critical sources of supply, insuring your attractiveness to skilled human resources, and controlling your future borrowing power. Your own people and your customer's people must both know your commitment. It should be verbalized in your standards of performance. It should also be evidenced in your allocations of your best talent and their time to your key customers.

3. *You must measure.* You must agree with your customer decision makers on the criteria you will use together to take periodic readings on the progress of improving customer profits. There can be no appreciation of accomplishment without knowledge in advance about how it will be determined. The criteria of performance and profit that will be used must be laid down at the start. So must the measurement tools that will be used to read the criteria. Just as good fences make good neighbors, good measuring standards make good partners.

Rules for Structuring Alliances

At all levels of a customer organization, key account partnerships are unusual unions. They are formed in mutual self-interest. They are sustained by adhering to specific rules that help maintain the joint objectives of both partners and, at the same time, advance their individual causes. All the rules conform to common sense. Yet it is not enough to assume that any representative can therefore partner with any customer simply by going about his or her business or by "being open and aboveboard" or by "treating your partner as you yourself would like to be treated." Partners must be treated as they themselves like to be treated.

The grandfather rule of partnering is to take a "we approach." What this does not mean is as important as what it does. It does not mean projecting yourself and your own needs onto your partner. "We" does not equal "me plus." It does not mean acting in a self-seeking manner and then giving your customer your best regards. It does not mean using the customer, manipulating the customer, or dazzling the customer with buzz words that may distract him or her from your personal motives.

To be a good ally means displaying attributes like these:

1. Add important values to your partners. Supply benefits that are not readily obtainable. Translate them into profit terms.

2. Be a dependable supplier of valuable benefits. Be reliable as an improver of customer profits. Let your partners be able to count on your contribution.

3. Understand your partners' expectations from your relationship and make sure you fulfill them. What your partners receive must be what they expect if they are to go on being your partners.

4. Educate your partners. Help them become more proficient in managing their operations. At the same time, help your partners become more efficient in educating you in the information you need to know to keep improving his or her proficiency.

5. Avoid surprises that delay or prevent the achievement of your partnership's objectives. Surprise indicates ineptitude in either your planning or your implementation. It also implies carelessness and lack of consideration for your partners.

6. Go beyond the responsibilities you have set for yourself. Take extra steps, show extra effort, and provide extra benefits of either a professional or personal nature.

Partnerships may seem to be made in Heaven, but they do not operate there. They do business in the real world, where conflict is inherent in every long-term relationship. A safe form of confrontation must be provided for the partners to work off frustrations—whether they originate inside the partnership or come from outside its boundaries—to express anxieties, and to test convictions. Devil's advocacy furnishes the safest way or resolving conflict.

You and your customer partners should agree to be each other's devil's advocates. Nothing should be sacred in its idea stage. Why this? Why not that? Why not both? Why either? Add this—what does that do? Take away that—is it an improvement? What can we combine, rearrange, sequence differently, simplify, or enlarge into a superproduct? What can we eliminate entirely?

Devil's advocates sharpen each other, hone their ideas to the most workable few, and keep their partnership keen, flexible, and stimulating. They give themselves the chance to go after each other in a nonthreatening way. Advocacy is constructive, not destructive. It builds successively on each partner's contributions, adding value as it goes. What emerges is a solution that has been hammered out in the context of the partnership itself. Both partners can subscribe to it, because both have participated in its creation. Neither partner can feel ignored or deprived of input. Nor is the end result likely to be the type of compromise that adulterates the expectations of both partners and leaves them feeling deprived instead of enhanced.

Preventing Departnering

Knowing how to structure partnerships is one half of the alliance equation. The other half is knowing how to prevent their destruction through the reverse process of departnering.

Departnering occurs when two conditions are met. An alliance that is incomplete or unfulfilled within itself is vulnerable. When a more promising partner appears, it succumbs. Many troubled partnerships linger on because both partners temporarily subscribe to the belief that "You know what you've got, but you don't know what you're going to get." As soon as one partner believes that what he or she is going to get is better, the partnership will end. In key account selling, this means that the customer will also be lost.

Because markets are tight communities, the loss of one key customer inevitably raises doubts, creates assumptions, and fosters anxieties that threaten the stability of other key customer relations. A domino effect can follow. The loss of one key partner or one key account will open the door to competitors who, even if they have not been a cause of your departnering, will want to take advantage of its effects. Furthermore, it may be impossible for you to replace the loss over the short term. In many industries, loss of a key piece of business means that you are out of consideration for a next chance for three to five years, when a customer's buying cycle cranks up again.

What leaves an alliance incomplete or causes it to be unfulfilled? There are two major factors that predispose eventual departnering:

1. *Divergent objectives.* Partnerships rest on similar ends. Both partners must have the same end result in mind before they partner, see the same end as being achieved while they are partnering, and be able to look back at the accomplishment of their ends as a consequence of the partnership.

It can be said that partnerships are known by the objectives the partners have in common. The eternal question of what two people see in each other is easily answered: They want to achieve the same objectives, and they perceive the partnership as the optimal means of reaching them. This is their hidden agenda.

A key account partnership is not a one-on-one situation. More accurately, it is a two-for-one relationship. Both partners share one objective—to improve the customer's profit. Unless this is accomplished, the sales representative's other objective of improving his or her own profit contribution will be impossible to attain. For this reason, the customer's objective must come first for both of them. It is not philanthropy but enlightened self-interest that makes it so.

When objectives diverge, or simply appear to be going off in different directions or diminishing in the conviction held by one of the partners, alliances atomize. A customer partner may acquire the belief that your representative is more interested in self-promotion to the customer's top tier than in merchandising the partnership. The customer partner may feel used, demeaned, and taken unfair advantage of by acting as a reference to help your representative further your business elsewhere. Your representative, on the other hand, may believe many of the same things about the customer partner. Whether such perceptions are true or not, they will have an erosive effect on the partnership.

Restating objectives and recommitting to them are essential elements in keeping partnerships on track. Objectives should be brought up for discussion at frequent intervals at the initiative of your representatives. A good time to introduce them is when progress is being measured against them. At some of these checkpoints, the original objectives may have to be downgraded, or perhaps they can benefit from unexpected progress by being increased. In either event, keeping them current will perpetuate their meaningfulness as the end results that both partners are working for.

2. *Unequal risk.* Partnerships are a means of reducing risk. Two parties can share the load, divide the responsibility, and parcel out the components of the task that would otherwise be borne by one or left undone. While the risk is reduced, it is never eliminated. It must be shared as equally as possible if the partnership is to be preserved. Otherwise, your partner may accuse you of "putting your hand out further than your neck."

No matter how hard your representatives try to bring into balance the risk of failing to improve customer profits, the customers will always be left with the major portion of exposure. They are exposed inside their own companies. They are exposed on their own and also on behalf of your representatives, whom they recommend to their own people. They are exposed to their topmost tier of management. In any business situation, there can be no riskier combination of exposures.

There is no question about it: Once customers commit themselves to work with you to improve their profit, they must be successful. It is no wonder that they will be ultrasensitive to their own inherent risk and to the support they receive from your representatives. They have a lot on the line.

Because customers bear the major share of a partnerships' risk, you must take on the major share of reducing the risk and providing the reassurance that it has indeed been reduced. You cannot have the same degree of risk as your customers. But you can provide a greater degree of risk calculation and limitation. This must be your equalizer.

You have several equalizing tools at your disposal. One is to be thorough in your fact finding and in putting together the data base on customer problems and opportunities. Another is to be diligent in obtaining feedback from your customers about their needs as they express them. A third is to manage your account review sessions with care so that deviations from objectives are caught early when they can be corrected, so that strategies can be revised to meet changed conditions, and so that opportunities can be capitalized when they are still fully available.

Suppose you fail to keep a partnership's objectives from diverging or its risks from being equalized—what then? The result is fairly predictable to forecast. Your customer will seek a new partner who meets two qualifications: a lowered risk and more harmonious objectives. While your partner is at it, he or she will be receptive to a seller who can deliver higher objectives. These may come in the form of greater profits, a more

productive product mix, or a broader range of options to
choose from in optimizing performance.

Improved objectives may also come from a quicker
flow of profits or productivity gains. New monies would
come in sooner or existing costs could be reduced in a
shorter period of time.

When objectives fall out of harmony, and the in-
equality of risk becomes uncomfortably oppressive, the
emergence of a new partner is inevitable. It invariably is
a lengthy process for customers to decide to bite the
bullet and open up a search, evaluate possibilities, and
then hold their breath while they make a selection. But it
always seems sudden to the sales representatives on
whom the boom is lowered. Their lack of awareness is
the proof of the pudding about how far the partners have
drifted apart.

The history of termination of customer-supplier and
client-consultant partnerships is filled with surprised suppliers and consultants. "Why, it was only yesterday"
they say, "that he was telling me what a great guy I
was—how much we had been through together, and how
he would always be indebted to me." If it was not "only
yesterday," it was "only last week" or "last month." The
epitaph is generally the same: How great it was. Meanwhile, for the new partner, the benediction is: How great
it is going to be.

Insuring Continuity

The ultimate criterion of partnership is that neither
partner can afford to let the other partner go. Each is too
valuable. Each represents too much profit potential.
Each embodies too much of an investment that promises
yet unrealized results.

Partners in a consultative alliance become invaluable to each other. They are priceless assets, impossible to replicate or replace. Their loss is the equivalent of a catastrophic failure. It is unthinkable.

How can your representatives become this sort of partner and insure the continuity of their key customer alliances? The following scenario provides the answer. It is taken from an actual dialog between a well-partnered customer and a would-be usurper of the consultant's role.

"I would like to work with you in the privileged position that Phil Smith of the Continental Group now enjoys."

"Phil privileges us. That is why he is privileged."

"Exactly what does Smith do for you that privileges you so much?"

"Phil helps us improve our profit more than we can improve it without him—more than we can improve it ourselves—more than we can improve it with anyone else in the functions of our business that he affects."

"I can affect those same functions. Our companies are directly competitive. I may be able to improve your profit every bit as much as he does."

"But he already is. The best you can say is that you may."

"How can I say I can unless you let me try?"

"I can't let you try until I know you can."

"Then how did Smith ever get started with you if he had to prove he could improve your profit before you let him?"

"That's how. He showed us how much profit he could improve. It was only then that we let him."

"I would like to show you how much profit I could improve. Then you would have a choice: Smith's company or mine."

"You said you might be able to improve our profit as much as Phil does. In that case, how could we choose between you? Making a choice is an expensive process. It involves many comparisons, many proofs, and many subjective determinations when all the facts are in. In order for us to consider replacing Phil, you would have to do better than he does for us . . . not just the same."

"How would it be if for every dollar of improved profit that Smith gets for you, I can give you an extra 10 cents?"

"That might not be enough to justify our making a change even if you could do it. And you realize that doing it once wouldn't be enough. You'd have to do it consistently. Otherwise we'd be better off with Phil."

"Well, how much better would be enough for you?"

"Before we could switch from Phil Smith with comfort and conviction, we'd probably have to have someone give us between 50 percent and 100 percent more profit. And again, they would have to do it consistently."

"All right. Suppose I can do that?"

"How would you go about it?"

"Because we want your business, we'd work harder. We'd be better motivated. We'd work smarter, too. We'd put our best brains against your problems. Besides, we have a better product. Your results would have to be better."

"But 50 percent to 100 percent better? That's a lot. Even Phil Smith hasn't been able to do that for us."

"That's the best reason in the world for you to switch."

"It may be the worst reason. It may be that Phil knows something that you don't know."

"What's that?"

"Our company. Our business. Our people. Our operating constraints. In one word—us."

Customer continuity can only be insured by customer knowledge. In the last analysis, it is who you know among top-tier customer decision makers and how much you know about their business operations that gives you insurance against departnering and in favor of lasting alliances. Your interpersonal abilities to penetrate top-tier customer management and the integrity of your customer data base are your two principal assets in creating and extending consultative relationships. Given these, you possess sales-making capacity at high margins. You also possess the consultant's positioning that insulates you from competitive thrusts to take you back down to vendor status.

For both you and your customer, alternatives to your alliance must be found wanting. The alternatives must be less improved profit, less shared knowledge about the customer's business, and lessened ability to prepare the customer to meet the future industry opportunities as one of its leaders.

Even in the best of cases, there can only be two possible answers to the question "What is the alternative to our alliance?" One could be another alliance. You must be able to nullify this response by knowing more about your customer's business and being better able to implement your knowledge to help improve customer profits. The other alternative is for the customer to seek remedy internally. You must once again be the better option.

How can you be better than your customers at solving their problems? This is where your experience and your ability must come into play. Their operating problems are only a part of their business. They are really in business to do something else—manufacture their own products, for example, and not to manage an inventory control system or invest their pension funds. On the other hand, solving one or more of their operating problems is the entire reason for the existence of your business. Their problems bring them costs. Solving them brings you profit. The customers' problems are seen by their people in the single environment of their own business. You see them from the environmental perspective of many companies. You see their similarities and differences, the common denominators of solutions, and the specific attributes that call for customized approaches that are one-of-a-kind.

Your key account customers have one overriding need: They must focus on the opportunities of their own business. Problems distract them. They detract from the profits that their opportunities provide. If an alliance with you can help free their energies from problems so they can seize their opportunities, and seize them more profitably, you have the natural foundation for a partnership in profit improvement.

The Alliance Contract

Top-tier alliances are implicit contracts. Although they are informal, they are operative because they are based on the mutual self-interest that is the foundation of all partnerships. Alliances can be aided and abetted by

Figure 2. Alliance contract.

Customer Decision Maker_____

Position_____

   Will partner with me in an alliance to (common objectives):

     1. _____

     2. _____

     3. _____

   Because of the following areas of mutual importance

   (common interests):

     1. _____

     2. _____

     3. _____

making them more explicit, especially in their young stages. The Alliance Contract illustrated in Figure 2 provides a self-disciplining method for planning and positioning each partnership at a top-tier level.

The contract requires key account sales representatives to define the two focal points that determine a partnership. One is the common objectives on which the allies must agree. The other is the common interests on which the objectives are based. Each of these categories should be spelled out in detail, and in quantified dollar units, on the contract.

A common objective can be to improve the profit contributed from the customer's operation by 5 percent, or $10,000, within the next 120 days. The underlying interests could be to help the customer solidify a career position as business function manager, increase the importance of the function as a money-maker in the plans of top management, and thereby make the function an improved candidate for further modernization. These are interests that can be held in unison by both a sales representative and his or her customer. The more solidified a customer partner becomes, the better purchaser the partner can be. The more contributory a function becomes, the better prospect it is for further sales that can yield even greater improvements.

No mention is made in the contract of the sales representative's self-interests. These would not be shared by the customer. Instead, the representative's interests must be achieved by meeting the customer's needs.

Key account sales representatives should "take out a contract" on every potential ally in top customer management, financial management, and the management of the business functions to which they sell. Contracts have two purposes. They provide a concretized platform from

Figure 3.   Alliance migration plan.

Customer/Division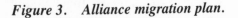

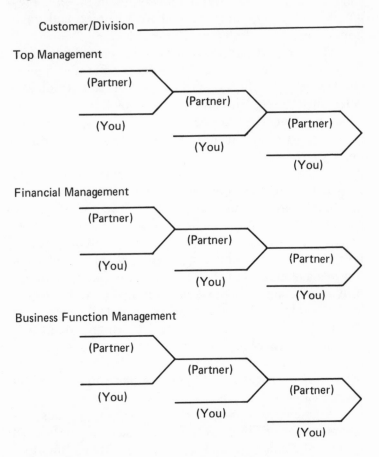

which partners can work together under the sales representative's leadership. They also furnish the jumping-off
places for migrating initial partnerships into successive
alliances. The Alliance Migration Plan shown in Figure 3
offers a method for projecting partnerships downrange
into the management chain, so that each alliance can lead
sequentially to others of mutual value.

4

Business Function Profiling

How to Target Customer Operations

The high margins that accrue from key account selling are your reward for knowing more about the customer operations you affect—and being able to improve them—than your competitors. Margins are merited by mastery of how a customer runs the business functions that are your sales targets. The more you know about them, and the better you are able to implement what you know into proposals for performing them more cost-effectively, the greater your value will be, and the higher the price you will deserve.

Key account selling is industry-dedicated. Within each industry, it is "function specific." Business functions in customer companies are your end users—your true markets. According to the way they operate, they throw off the costs that you can reduce or do away with entirely. They can add new sales revenues or productivity if you can show them how. Your customer business functions are the sources of the problems you will have to solve and the showcases where the value of your solutions will give testimony to your capabilities. Scoping their ways of operating should therefore be your constant preoccupation.

If you are going to sell in a consultative manner, the operating of customer business functions will be the subject matter of your consultation. The only alternative is to talk about your own processes and the products or services they produce. In that case, you will be talking to the purchasing tier, and you will be selling on a basis of competitive performance and price. Your opportunity for high margins will have vanished.

In order to know a customer's business functions from an operating perspective and from the point of view of their financial structure, you will have to get inside customer businesses. Generic knowledge of a function based on industrywide generalizations is important and useful. But it is insufficient. Norms and averages can be extremely helpful, especially if they are used as jumping-off places to learn the specifics of individual customer operations. But by themselves they are insufficient. The actual facts and figures of a competitive company's function may be intriguing and suggestive. But they are insufficient because, as every customer will tell you, "My business is different."

The only business function profile a customer will recognize is his or her own. It is also the profile the customer guards most zealously. There is good reason for this. Little perceived value comes from releasing functional operating or cost information. There are many people and organizations that can use it detrimentally. Conversely, there are few if any who might use it helpfully. If you want to qualify as a helpful source, you must first pay your dues. You must do homework on your customer businesses. Then, based on what you have learned and how well you can apply it, you may be invited to propose improvements.

The ability to profile a customer business function is an essential skill to sell at the top tier. In customer functions, you will find the problems you will propose to solve when you take them to the top. Unless you know the nature of these problems, their importance, their financial values, and the language in which customer top management discusses them, you will be talking to yourself when you get there.

There are three ways to profile a business function that correspond with top-tier management's own ways of scoping it. One is to examine its context within your customer company. The second is to evaluate its operations. The third is to analyze its principal areas of intensivity: what it depends on the most for its operations. There is a fourth way, too, that is important for you. It is the need to understand a function's decision makers.

Examining a Function's Context

Every customer operating function is a miniature business. The research and development function is a science laboratory. The product engineering function is a craft workshop. The manufacturing function is a machine shop and assembly line. The sales function is a distribution organization. Each function is tolerated by top-tier management of the parent company because management has decided that it is more cost-effective to own its capabilities than to buy them from the outside. They all operate at a cost. In some companies, manufacturing is expected to produce a gross margin. Sometimes the information processing function will market portions of its data base and bring in revenues. But in general, only the sales function is regularly charged with producing major profits.

Because every business function is a cost center, it has the potential ability of running up expenses that are intolerable—that is, they significantly erode profits. Cost control becomes a paramount consideration with every customer to prevent this from happening. Management thinks of this mission as controlling a function's contribution to cost.

This is the financial context in which customer business functions exist. You must know how these functions fit inside your customer business—that is, how much cost they generate—as if they were your own. From a sales point of view, they are your own: your own market.

Evaluating a Function's Operations

Business functions are processes. All processes have a flow. They have a beginning, a middle, and an end. Manufacturing begins with raw materials and ends with finished products in inventory. Data processing begins with raw information from many sources and ends with summaries, compilations, and reports. There are costs at both ends. In between, there is nothing but costs.

Every functional process has its critical few points. There are the places, times, and activities in the course of the process where its major contributions to value are made and where its major costs are incurred. In some operations, these are referred to as choke points. Unless they work in the most cost-effective manner, the output from the entire process may be throttled.

You and your representatives should be able to chart the flow of the key customer processes you affect from start to finish. You should be able to assign appropriate costs to the critical few points that control the process and be able to prescribe the optimal remedy for the portion of these costs that you can help reduce or enable your customer to rule out entirely.

Some of your remedies will be therapeutic. They will lower an existing cost. Other remedies will be curative. They will alter a process, combine it with another, or eliminate it from the flow. In still other cases, your remedy will be to change the architecture of a process so radically that a completely new set of cost centers will result.

A process flow is diagrammed in simplified format in Figure 4. It shows the movement of activities and the accumulation of their costs in a customer's receivables collection process from their inception after 30 days outstanding through the end of the process. At each stage, new costs are added. Most of them are direct costs. When sales representatives must be diverted from making new sales to collecting payments for sales already made, both direct costs and opportunity costs are generated.

If the collection process shown in the figure can be foreshortened by even one step—and therefore made more economical by the elimination of one added cost—a true monetary advantage can be brought to the customer. Its net effect will be to improve the contribution of profit that can be made by the receivables collection process.

Analyzing a Function's Intensivity

All customer business functions are intensive in their use of one or more resources of operation. The sales function is labor-intensive. Research and development is technology-intensive as well as labor-intensive at an extremely costly and highly educated level of labor. Manufacturing may be energy-intensive.

Figure 4. Receivables collection process flow.

BUSINESS FUNCTIONS

Credit & Collection >>> Credit & Collection >>> Credit & Collection >>> Legal

>>> Outside Collection
Agency

TIME   COSTS

30 DAYS	60 DAYS	90 DAYS	120 DAYS
1. Collection costs (+) $____	1. Collection costs $____	(+) 1. Collection costs $____	(+) 1. Collection costs $____
	2. Opportunity cost of unavailable funds $____	2. Opportunity cost of unavailable funds $____	2. Opportunity cost of unavailable funds $____
		3. Opportunity cost of lost sales $____	3. Opportunity cost of lost collections $____

Plant construction and equipment modernization are investment-intensive.

The areas in which a function is intensive define the type and volume of its cost configuration. They set the targets for your sales thrust. If a process you affect is labor-intensive, you will want to focus your sales on reducing the amount of labor required, reducing the level of training that is currently required for the workforce so that lower-cost labor may be substituted, replacing labor with technology, substituting external contract labor for internal workforces, or improving the productivity of labor so that an additional workforce will not have to be hired, and each unit of labor can increase its contribution to profit for each dollar of its cost.

In dealing with technology intensivity, newer forms of science such as electronic controls may contribute more cost effectiveness than electromechanical controls. On the other hand, increasing the intensivity of labor may be more cost-effective than upgrading a technology.

Your consultative expertise will necessarily fall within the intensive areas of your key customer processes. You will be an assembly process expert for labor-intensive customers and a distribution process expert for sales-intensive customers. In everything you do, however, you will be expert in either reducing investment intensivity or increasing its ability to generate a more extensive return.

Evaluating a Function's Decision Makers

Decision makers preside over every business function. He or she is usually the function's manager. Influencers reinforce his or her decisions or argue for contrary determinations. Other decision makers may be found at key steps in the function's processes. Some of them are functionaries. They make a process go. Others are managers. They watch over its costs. These are the primary players you must take into consideration when you profile a business function.

Primary players directly affect a function. Outside their circle are the secondary players who are affected by their decisions. These may be primary players in other functions. Taken together, they represent the deciding voices in the acceptance or rejection of your proposals.

You cannot claim to know a customer's business unless you know the decision makers, where they can be found, and where they set their minimum thresholds for making affirmative buying recommendations in your favor. How much improved profit meets each decider's minimum criteria? How shortly must it start flowing in order to be regarded as soon enough? How certain must it be? How much proof is required to be convincing? What kinds of proof are most meaningful?

Only when you know things like these about key customer decision makers can you work with them in a consultative manner. Only then can you deal with them on a businesslike basis as opposed to simply a buyer-seller relationship. Knowing decision makers means knowing what is decisive for them when it comes time to invest their limited funds with you.

Scoping the Options

When you make your initial penetration of targeted customer operations, you already know a good deal about the business functions into which you sell. Even if you have only been vending, you have learned about at least three major subjects. In terms of products and services, you probably understand what has already been done by your key account customers to make their functions more cost-effective. You know what they have purchased, from whom, for how much, and what the results have been.

You also probably know what other companies in your customer's industry have done to solve similar problems. Some of them may be your customers; others may be prospects. From whom have they bought? At what price? With what performance benefits? Third, you undoubtedly know something about upcoming new products and services that might create a difference in customer operations that would far exceed their cost or the best performance contributions that can be achieved today.

Just by being in business, you know most of these things. As a consultative seller, you must know something more about customer operations. From the outset, you must know the options available for improved customer profit. You will have to study customer business functions so well that you can prescribe the optimal mix of cost-reducing options and value-adding options for each one of their main problems.

1. *Cost-reducing options*. When you screen a business function, you must be able to learn its costs on a before-and-after tabulation. What are its costs right now, today? You must then be able to prescribe the best mix of available options that can accomplish some or all of three objectives. They must leave a customer with fewer dollars in costs. They must take a shorter time to get costs down than other options. They must be highly certain to perform.

2. *Value-adding options*. At the same time you screen a customer business function for its costs, you should also profile the options for adding new dollar

Figure 5.   Value/cost matrix.

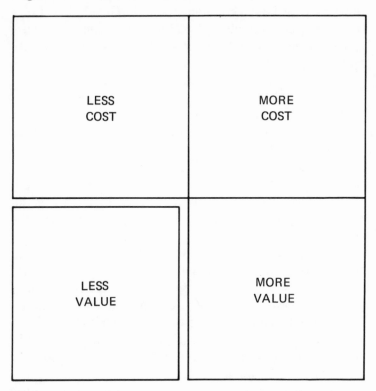

values. How can its revenue-generating operations be strengthened? By how much? How can its productivity be magnified? By how much, and what is the dollar value of the increase? Here again, you must be able to prescribe the best available mix of options that can accomplish these improvements. They must bring a customer more money. They must bring it in a shorter time than other improvements. They must be highly certain to perform.

There is no such thing as the universal solution. No option to produce less cost for a customer or to add more value will fit all customers, even if the function being penetrated is the same throughout an industry. In Figure 5, you will see a Value/Cost Matrix composed of the four options that are your building blocks in scoping a customer business function as a sales target. You can contribute less or more cost. You can contribute less or more value. The matrix should be read like this:

1. If you can combine more value at less cost, you have the ideal solution.
2. If you can combine more value even at more cost, you may also have an ideal solution, as long as the added value sufficiently exceeds the added cost.

Either of these options represents consultative selling strategy. You should have them in mind as you approach a customer operation with the objective of learning its costs and the values it will need from you. By knowing what your options are, you will be better able to select the relevant customer data you need and to structure it to meet your eventual profit-improvement recommendations. In order to come out with what you want, you must go in with the framework of your eventual sales strategy.

Problem/Solution Definition

A problem that is properly defined is supposed to be two-thirds of the way to solution. The Business Function Problem-Definition Statement shown in Figure 6 is designed to make it necessary to qualify and quantify a problem in advance of attempting its solution.

The definition statement requires a business function problem to be qualified in narrative terms: what kind

76 KEY ACCOUNT SELLING

Figure 6.   Business function problem-definition statement.

Customer/Division_____

Line of Business_____

Business Function_____

Problem Qualification

_____

_____

_____

Problem Quantification

  Contribution to Cost

1. _____ = $ _____

2. _____ = _____

3. _____ = _____

4. _____ = _____

                Total cost   =====================

of problem it is for the customer, where it is located in the customer's operations, what its effects are in the contribution it makes to costs and performance, what other problems it is connected to or is influenced by. Then the statement asks for an itemization of the dollar contributions of cost that are currently being made by the problem on an item-by-item basis. The problem's total cost is summarized as the statement's conclusion.

Figure 7 is the follow-on to problem definition. It shows an outline form for the creation of an optimal solution to the customer's problem. It summarizes the problem in descriptive and financial terms and then sketches the essential components of the solution that will deliver the best benefits. The solution outline and the problem statement will form the core of each profit improvement proposal that will be developed to make top-tier penetration.

Profiling a Target Function

To vend, you need to know your own costs. To sell in a consultative manner, you need to know customer function costs. To vend, you need to know your own sales opportunities. To sell as a consultant, you need to know customer sales opportunities. Realizing that you must come up with a cost-reducing or value-adding op-

Figure 7.   Solution outline.

Customer/Division_____

   Line of Business_____

   Business Function_____

Problem Qualification Summary_____

_____

Problem Quantification Total $_____

Solution

   1. _____

   2. _____

   3. _____

   4. _____

   5. _____

   6. _____

   7. _____

      Total Performance Improvement $_____

tion, how can you learn a customer's current costs in the business functions that are important to you? How can you get a fix on the customer's unachieved sales potential?

In your profiling of target functions, how can you quantify with reasonable accuracy the operating problems and opportunities that will form the base of your key account penetration plans?

You will need to begin the development of three data bases, banks of information that will become the basic resources for top-tier selling at key accounts:

1. An *industry data base* cn each of the industries in which you serve key customers.
2. A *customer data base* on each key account customer you serve in an industry.
3. A *customer's customer data base* on your key accounts' key accounts.

From your industry data base, you will learn the average costs, average profits on sales, average inventories and receivables, and other industry norms that are the standards for its member companies. The information in each of your key customer data bases will allow you to compare customer performance against industry averages. In categories where a customer falls below the norms, you may find sales opportunity.

Your individual customer data bases will teach you the concentration and distribution of customer costs. Where do they bunch up? Are these the same places for the industry as a whole? How heavy are they? Are they typical for the industry? What are their trends—are they rising every year, or are they coming under control? What variable factors affect them most significantly?

Your customer data bases will also provide you with knowledge of where potential new sales opportunities may be found. These may be for improved existing products, new products, combined products, new or enhanced services, superproducts, or systems. How can your customers sell more? How can they sell at higher prices? How can they extend sales into closely adjacent markets? How can they invade new markets that offer superior profit opportunity? How can they anticipate or turn back a competitive thrust?

In order for you to "know your customers' business," you must know more than the performance characteristics and their cost contributions of the internal business functions that you can affect. You must know the key customers they sell to. They are the customers' opportunity. Their needs are also the determining pressures that cause many of the customers' processes to operate the way they do: to manufacture the kinds of products they make, to advertise and sell the way they do, to communicate inside and outside their businesses with the telecommunications technologies they use. Only when you know your customers' customers can you understand the complete spectrum of the consultative relationship that will be available to you—the full range of their costs that can be reduced and their sales opportunities that can be enlarged.

The essential elements of information you will need to know about your customers' customers are exactly the same as the data you must develop on your customers themselves. You will have to learn the major cost areas your customers affect in their own key account businesses and the main sales opportunities they help them achieve. Do your customers have mature products that you can help them rebrand, as discussed in Appendix 2? Unless your customers have been selling in a consultative manner to their key accounts, it is unlikely they will have this information. In all probability, they have been vending. They will know their customers' price and performance specifications, their customer decision makers' favorite jokes and luncheon menus, but little else. You will have to learn together what you both need to know.

The joint development of information is one of the strongest bonds for partnering. Shared discovery is an alliance of adventurers, adding new values to themselves and to each other. Joint research can also be cost sharing, another partnering act. At best, your key customers will realize that they will have to expand their knowledge of their own customers if they are going to be able to help you help them improve profits. They will, of course, also be able to use customer knowledge to sell consultatively themselves. At worst, you may have to suggest a cooperative starter survey to demonstrate its value.

Learning from Multiple Industry Sources

Getting into the cost structure of an industry and its customers is a two-stage effort. If you have never done it before, it is a front end-loaded undertaking. Once you have structured your data bases, it is simple and inexpensive to keep them up to date. The first stage is to learn as much as you can from the multiple sources that are always available without going to your customers themselves. Then, when you take on the second and third stages that deal specifically with your accounts, you will have two advantages: You will already know a great amount, so you will have less to ask of customers, and you will have a meaningful framework on which to hang the information they share with you.

In addition to the ubiquitous publications and knowledgeable career professionals of the United States

government—especially the Department of Commerce—
six additional sources can be turned to for your needs to
know the costs and revenue potentials of customers in a
key industry:

1. *The people and information resources inside your
own company* are the first and most obvious source.
Some of your people may have been recruited from customer industries. Some may even have worked for key
customers. Others may have participated in market research studies that sought information that can now be
related to your consultative needs. If you maintain a library, its periodicals and publications can be culled for
data—especially the trade magazines of your key industries. Your librarian can be a valuable aide in obtaining
published information of all types.

2. *Trade associations* in your customer industries
are staffed by people who usually devote their lifetimes
to their trade. They know many generalities and often
specific information about individual companies. They
know the main leaders in the industry and can introduce
you. Their associations also maintain industry libraries
and computerized data bases.

3. *Security analysts* are professional researchers of
specific industries who are employed by brokerage
houses to follow their industries over long periods of
time. They publish updated industry analyses that evaluate growth potential, highlight the major factors that determine profits and costs, and define trends that can
forecast opportunities. Many analysts will provide personal counsel on a quid pro quo basis.

4. *Industry experts and consultants* can be retained
on a one-shot or periodic basis to lay down a foundation
for understanding an industry's process flows and its cost
structure. They can also be helpful in estimating the impact of your technology on customer costs and produc-

tivity, keeping you in touch with competitive technologies, and exchanging information on business function problems that an industry as a whole and its individual customer companies are afflicted by and the strategies they are currently implementing, or plan to implement, to solve them.

5. *Other suppliers* who sell noncompetitive products and services to the same business function decision makers at your key accounts may have acquired knowledge of customer process costs and sales opportunities they will share with you. They will probably approach the knowledge you seek from the bias of their own interests. This may make their information peripheral to your needs. Nonetheless, you may be able to translate it or project it onto the way your own business cuts into customer costs.

6. *Noncustomer companies or non-key account customers* in the same industry are sometimes easier to approach in a quest for generalizable information than your own customers. They operate the same business functions. Their costs tend to cluster in the same critical few choke points. The potential sales opportunities of the industry affect them in the same way as they intrigue your key accounts. Even though their businesses are different in many ways from the business of any one of your own key customers, enough clues will generally be found to make their cultivation worthwhile.

Learning from Public Customer Sources

After you have done your homework with multiple industry information sources and before you approach your key customers themselves, there is an important intermediate step. Every customer company reveals publicly many facts about its existing operations and plans for forthcoming investments or divestitures. These revelations are invaluable to you because they are authentic. They come from the horse's mouth. You should unfailingly investigate them, not only as you start up your learning curve in the transition to top-tier selling but on a continuing basis. There are two major sources from which you can learn what customer companies are proclaiming or complaining about themselves:

1. *Annual reports and 10-K reports* give you access to information on your customers' current financial condition and its trends, their objectives, and the major problems and constraints they are encountering in achieving them, how and where they are introducing new technologies and systems to alter the intensive nature of their operations, ways and areas where productivity improvement is important, new product developments and the changes they may make in the market share configurations of existing products. The annual report is the form this information takes for presentation to shareholders. The 10-K version is far more detailed and far less florid, since it is put together for the Securities and Exchange Commission.

2. *Presidential speech transcripts* are reprinted in the *Wall Street Transcript. Forbes, Business Week,* and other business media often interview chief executive officers. CEOs are increasingly appearing for interviews on network television and cable programming. The interview format creates a wide-ranging agenda for comment, sometimes eliciting off-the-cuff remarks and spontaneous declarations that can give you important insights. These will also provide useful conversational tidbits when you sit down with your customer decision makers in the third stage of your information gathering.

Learning from Customer Sources

When you have learned as much as you can from industry sources and from sources your key customers make public, then and only then are you ready to confront your customers themselves to learn the rest of what you need to know. By this time, you will have less to ask. You will not have to request anything you do not require. You will be able to phrase your negotiations in "customer language," which is the jargon of each industry. You will be able to initiate discussion by recapitulating what you already know instead of asking for help up front. You will have shown commitment to your customer businesses by your willingness to invest homework time and effort in advance of a payback. And in the course of your studies, many ideas will occur to you for improving customer profit that will provoke further information from their decision makers as you introduce them into your negotiations.

No information source on a customer's business can equal the customer's people themselves. They speak with authority for two reasons. They have the inside track on customer operations; indeed, they originate much of the information themselves. Second, the information they believe is gospel. Right or wrong, their "facts" are the only facts. Their numbers are the only hard, firm numbers. Their concept of costs are the costs you will have to work with. Their view of unfulfilled opportunities are the opportunities you will have to help them seize.

In an ideal world, customer facts and figures would be open to you for your asking. Every now and then it happens in exactly this way. A vendor supplier sits down before the top-tier managers of a key account customer and presents generalized narrative benefits of working together in a two-tier manner. For the work they will do at the top tier, the supplier proposes a partnership based on consultative selling strategies. The supplier reveals minimal customer knowledge and asks to be provided with the rest. The customer somehow senses the value of the benefits and agrees.

This is called the Phil Smith Approach, in honor of the first man known to have successfully accomplished it the first and only time he tried it.

The other approach is called the consultative selling approach, because it is the strategy that almost always must be used. It is also known as the hard way. It is the usual strategy, because customers do not give internal operating information and its financial implication to vendors—especially to vendor sales representatives. As a result, a vicious circle is set up. A vendor needs inside customer information to switch from vending to top-tier consultation. Yet customers do not release inside information to vendors. Without the information, a vendor will forever remain a vendor. How can the circle be broken?

The only way that experience proves workable is for vendors to first learn as much as possible from industry and public customer sources about customer cost problems and sales opportunities. Then they can adopt a quasi-consultative role as a halfway step between vending and consulting, in which they share the data they have, offer tentative proposals based on their implications, and thereby motivate their customers to share the rest of what they need to know in order to achieve the proposed profits.

In this twilight zone between vending and consulting, vendors are not asking customers to give them information. They are inviting customers to trade information with them the way consultants do with their clients.

Trading is acceptable, where giving is not, because trading is rewarded on the spot with a return of equal or greater value.

To make the quasi-consultative approach work on your initial customer profiling, several requirements must be rigidly adhered to:

1. You must bring something to the party. You cannot come empty-handed. Your knowledge of a customer's industry and business must show evidence of effort and intelligence. Your tentative suggestions for proposals by which customer profits can be improved should demonstrate an appreciation of the customer's rank order of problems and your creativity in solving them.

2. You must be careful in trying to bend industry generalizations to fit an individual customer's own situation. Industry norms and averages are useful as points of comparison with a customer's performance. They should never be used as if they represent the customer's performance. Never use norms from other industries or even from other companies in a customer's industry as if they were customer norms.

3. You must be devastatingly honest about what you have not been able to learn and therefore do not know about a customer's business. When you construct a tentative proposal, you can leave these areas blank. As a second option, you can insert admittedly soft numbers for assumed cost figures. If you can use assumptions, you should try to come as close as possible to your best estimate of what a true figure would be. Then you should deliberately overestimate each customer cost item and deliberately underestimate the value of your solutions.

4. In your trial proposals, you must be able to show dollar benefits for a customer that meet his or her threshold of what is significant. Unless you can do this, the customer will have no incentive to trade information

with you. Partnering must promise a clear reward. The customer must believe it to be achievable by working together, and must also be able to visualize continuing the relationship after the first success.

5. You must make it simple for a customer to agree to trade business knowledge with you. This means that you should require as little information as possible. It also means that you should not require any information that a customer knows is publicly available about his or her business. You should not ask for major allocations of customer resources to further your work together. Your partnering requests should involve the fewest possible customer people, their time, and expense.

6. You must believe mightily in what you propose and that you can improve a customer's profit to the extent you claim. Your conviction will be contagious. It will be tested by customer decision makers who have never worked with you before—or with any supplier—in a consultative manner. Their comfort level in going ahead will be reinforced by the assurance you convey and the degree of support from your own resources that you are willing to commit.

Asking for Rights Before Proving Rewards

The quasi-consultative approach proposes a probable reward, shows the size of the up-front investment to arrive at it, and asks for a customer contribution of knowledge to firm up the exact dimensions of the reward. Sometimes vendors try a shortcut. They lack the unique human resources to create a consultative partnership from a standing start along the lines of the Phil Smith Approach. They also lack the dedication to do sufficient homework, or perhaps they feel they do not have adequate skills or time to first study customer industries and businesses on their own. Their approach is to ask customers for the right to study their businesses on the chance that ways and means of improving profits will be found.

Regardless of how customers respond to this approach—and customers occasionally react with favor, especially smaller companies who have not had their operations already studied to a fare-thee-well—it demeans suppliers. It depositions them from any pretension of being consultative. It fixes suppliers at the level of graduate students performing summer internships.

There are two principal risks to asking for the right to make a study before proving or even suggesting a reward. One is that studies that begin from ground zero range unnecessarily wide in search of targets. This involves many customer people, interrupting their work and increasing the chance that more than a few of them will be inconvenienced or antagonized enough to complain. Some may refuse to participate. Others may think the approach is naive. These are frequently the same people who will have to be partnered with if a consultative relationship is eventually established. It is not likely they will readily perceive the vendor as an equal.

The second risk is that even good results from such studies will be downgraded by the customers' top-management tier. The most typical criticism is something like this: "All they told us is what we told them." Since customers know they have provided all the information that goes into a study, they regard the data base that results as their possession. There is no sense of participation in its evolution. As a result, there is no felt need to reward the vendor for what customers believe they themselves have done for the vendor—rather than the other way around.

Asking for the right to study a customer's operations should be a last resort. It should never be a strategy of first choice. When a study is undertaken, it should be minimally disruptive and tightly managed for limited objectives to supplement what you already know. Its duration should be extremely short and should never exceed its alloted time.

Managing Your Business Function Knowledge

The phasing of your emergent expertise in the business functions you affect in key customer accounts will take place in this type of sequence:

1. You will know a little about one operation in one customer company in one industry.
2. You will know a lot about that one operation in that customer company.
3. Your will know a little about another operation in the same customer company, as you will be invited to migrate your profit-improvement strategy to another aspect of the same business function or to another function that you can affect.
4. You will know a little about the same operation in a second customer company, as you penetrate other key accounts in the same industry.
5. You will know a lot about that same operation in several customer companies. You will be storing their facts and figures in your APACHE data bases. Your expertise in bringing profit improvement to the operation will spread throughout the industry.
6. You will acquire similar data bases and expertise for improving the profit contribution of other

operations in the same business function and in
other business functions in the industry.
7. You will extend your knowledge and repute to
other industries.

This is the capsule history of how major corporations have managed their customer knowledge, extending it from operation to operation within a business
function, then to other business functions, then to other
customer companies in the same industry, and then to
other industries. In order to grow their key account sales
at high margins, they have marketed their knowledge of
customer business problems and opportunities. On the
surface, they have been selling profit-improving solutions. But the underlying value has been their understanding of customer problems. They appear as solution
experts. At rock bottom, however, they are process-
smart, operations-smart, function-smart—that is,—cus-
tomer-smart. Only then can they be smart suppliers.

As you learn how to manage your customer knowledge resources, you will discover two truths. No customer wants to be first with anything new. Yet as soon as
something new produces superior results, every customer wants to retain it on an exclusive basis. These
paradoxical attitudes will be reflected as you take the
first steps from vending to consultative selling. Finding
the first customer to work with—to let you inside hereto-
fore proprietary operations—will be more difficult than
finding the second. Yet working with a second customer
in the same industry may also be difficult, because the
first customer will want to monopolize your function-
profiling skills and profit-improving strategies.

In spite of these initial constraints, you will know
you have achieved consultant recognition in a customer
industry when a remarkable event occurs. You will be

invited by customers to profile their business functions—
not to bid on their business but to study its cost structure
and its sales opportunity. At that point, your knowledge
of industry norms will come importantly into play. Once
you have captured the knowledge of their processes,
your proposals for improvement will follow naturally.
After all, who will be better equipped?

What you know about customer functions will not
be what you sell. But what you sell will always be based
on what you know.

In many sales organizations, realization is accom-
panied by pain as the balance of power swings from
products and pricing specialists to customer operations
specialists as they move into consultative selling to top-
tier management of their key accounts. Product knowledge will always be preeminent at the vendor's
purchasing tier. But a sales organization will be perma-
nently welded into position there until it acquires the
customer data that enable it to move up. The short-run
agonies of change must be balanced against the long-term
agonies of decreasing margins, increasing competitive
parity, and rising costs that can never be retrieved by
price. The difference between top margins at the top tier
and eroding margins at the purchasing tier is in what you
know and who you know in your key accounts.

5

Sales Opportunity Data Basing

How to Generate Customer Proposals

In key account penetration, your proposals should originate at the same source where they will end—with your customers. They should come out of the customers' businesses first, authentically immersed in their problems, and then go back into their businesses carrying the added value of your solutions. Key account proposing is closed-circuit proposing. The customer starts and finishes the process. You are the intermediary.

To say the same thing in another way: profit improvement proposals are born in customer data. From the data, you learn how to qualify and quantify customer problems. You learn the mix of their current solutions. You learn the changes your own solutions can make in customer costs or, as they may refer to it, their allocation of resources. You learn the most receptive entry points to penetrate in order to propose your solutions and partner with the decision makers who stand guard over your entry.

Your key account data base speaks for your customers inside your own business. It represents their needs, matches your benefits with their needs, and assigns dollar values to the application of your benefits to their needs. It allows your key account representatives' proposals to come out of the real world of their customer businesses instead of an imaginary world of what your representatives believe their customers "should" or "must" need, want, or desire.

Without access to this kind of customer data, you cannot sell in a consultative manner. Without a way for your sales representatives to use the data as their proposal-making partner, you cannot sell consultatively in the most cost-effective manner.

The relation of consultative selling strategies to customer data is a dependent one. Lacking customer knowledge, sales representatives must fall back to being vendors who are forced to sell from the only knowledge they have—namely, price-performance knowledge about their products.

Since consultative selling proposals are entirely dependent on customer data, and since customer data depend on a structure for their accurate, timely, and creative use, a data base is required as the centerpiece of your key account penetration.

The data base must do more than merely store customer problem information and pair it up with your solutions. It must do more than be accessible and retrievable. Structured into a system, it must be able to act as a computerized partner of your key account representatives. In concert together, they will generate the proposals that will initiate and broaden your penetration at the top customer tiers of your key accounts. In return, each proposal should develop new information for your data base that will provide the basis for additional proposals, and so on in an endless cycle.

Figure 8. Information inflow-outflow model.

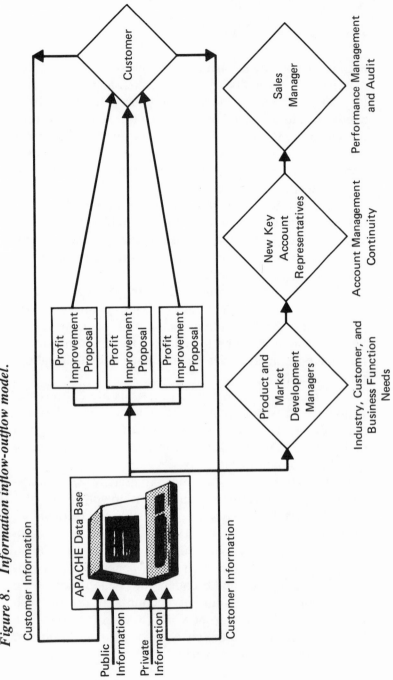

Customer Information

Public Information

Private Information

Customer Information

APACHE Data Base

Profit Improvement Proposal

Profit Improvement Proposal

Profit Improvement Proposal

Customer

Sales Manager

New Key Account Representatives

Product and Market Development Managers

Performance Management and Audit

Account Management Continuity

Industry, Customer, and Business Function Needs

This reciprocating system is illustrated in Figure 8. The data base is shown as the origin for proposal generation and the depository for new customer knowledge. Three other applications of the customer information that is in the data base are also indicated: its use by product and market development managers as a reservoir of customer needs, its use by new key account representatives to maintain your continuity of operating effectiveness on an account, and its use at the sales management level to manage the performance of your sales teams and audit their achievements against their plans.

Identifying Top-Tier Entry Points

Entry into a customer's top tier is provided for you by the existence of a business function problem that is profitable for you and the customer to solve.

When the job of key account selling is analyzed, most of its total time allocation is normally spent identifying the location of entry points that meet this definition. This part of the sales representative's work is a form of investigative reporting. It involves lining up sources, tracking down leads, checking them out, and then doing heavy-duty spadework. At this point, the sales representative is a long way from standing before a customer, selling.

The next largest expenditure of time is spent internally trying to get the cooperation of sales support services: customer service, manufacturing, data processing, credit, financial consultation, and so on. This part of the sales representative's work is a form of legal plea bargaining. It involves negotiation, compromise, and tradeoffs of past obligations for present favors. At this point, the sales representative is still a long way from standing before a customer, selling.

Selling, which is the job of your sales representatives, takes up the smallest share of their total time.

An APACHE data base can help reverse the ratio between selling and nonselling time by identifying the most profitable entry points for your representatives at the outset of their penetration-planning process. It can also shortcut their time spent on gaining internal cooperation by incorporating some of the work of financial consultation in quantifying the values of the customer profits they will be able to improve, by providing current credit information on key accounts, and in other similar ways.

Relieved of the up-front delays of entry point identification, your sales representatives can start the selling cycle sooner and thereby shorten its overall length. They can also start it smarter. The customer information that goes into a data base will generally be the product of many minds, both internal and outside. It will come from the personal experiences of people familiar with the account, from the account itself, from public sources in the customer's industry and the investment community—a far wider range of sources than any individual sales representative can ever cover.

An APACHE data base offers more than just information. It offers authentic information. It offers it faster than conventional sources of customer information and presents it in such a way that related needs can be combined and comprehensive problems built up from them. It offers information in words, numbers, and graphic formats such as computer-generated charts, tables, and diagrams that can be directly incorporated into a profit improvement proposal.

Increasing the amount of time your key account representatives spend before their top-tier decision makers will yield two advantages. By the law of averages, they will sell more. Their hits will improve. Second, they will learn more about customer problems from the source of this information, upper and upper middle customer management. This new knowledge will then be able to fertilize their data base to make it even more complete, more authentic, and more productive of sales proposals.

Structuring the Customer Data Base

Consultative data are live data. Like profit, customer data are a function of time. In order for the data to be accurate, they must be current. To be useful in proposing improvements in key account profitability, they must be structured in a format that makes them easy to get at and from which it is logical to work.

Customer data bases that can act as your sales representatives' partners in creating profit proposals must share the following characteristics:

Industry-dedicated. If you serve one industry, your data base will be dedicated to that industry. If you are organized into market centers, as discussed in Appendix 3, this will be a natural fit. If you serve multiple industries, you must have a separately dedicated data base for each industry, just as if it were your only one. In this way, you replicate your customers' perceptions about the peculiarities, the individualities, and the idiosyncrasies of their businesses. You learn to think in the same industry terms that they do, keep alert to the same industry trends and conditions, understand the same industry constraints, and acquire similar industry sensitivities.

Operations-centered. If you serve one division or one function of your key customer businesses, the customer and the division or function are synonymous. Your data base can be organized along division or functional lines. If you serve multiple types of divisional businesses within your customer organizations, or multiple business functions, your data bases will have to be organized by specific lines of business and specific business functions for each customer. The customer is no longer definable as the account as a whole. Instead, "the customer" is actually several individual operations managers, each of whose businesses you must know.

Problem-oriented. Each customer data base must focus on the problems that will be your prime selling targets. These problems will conform to three criteria:

1. They are important to your customers. This means that, operationally and financially, they are adversely affecting customer productivity, denying them added sales, and unnecessarily inflating costs.

2. They will be profitable for customers to solve. This means that the total cost of implementing a solution will be less than the continuing cost of tolerating the problem over a "useful life" of three to five years. It also means that the profit from the solution must exceed or at least equal the profit from investing the same dollar resources in comparable alternate ways.

3. They will be profitable for you to solve. This means that you can sell the solution at a high margin. It also means that the solution will generate the improved customer profit you have promised so that you will be able to upgrade it and migrate it—and so that you will not have to deplete your margins by providing remedial service, repair, and replacement under warranty.

Into this mix composed of customer industry information, customer operations information, and customer problem information must be added the one element of information that is not derived from the customer: your solution to the problems in your customer's business functions.

The act of inserting your solutions into a customer

data base on a problem-by-problem basis unifies your two businesses. It forms the basis for your partnership as problem solvers.

Your solutions should be entered into a customer data base in two forms:

1. *Your systems for solving customer problems.* Each product, service, and system you offer should be included as part of your internal information. Its features and benefits should be itemized, together with their symbiotic effects when two or more products or services are combined in a system. Each system should be defined according to its regular and optional component parts. Every offering should be correlated to the customer business functions it affects. Sequential upgrading modules should be itemized so that the contribution of each product or system can be examined from its simplest state through its most comprehensive form. Customer business functions to which it can most naturally migrate should also be specified.

2. *Your system values.* Each product, service, and system should have four values attached to it. The first three are internally known. One is its cost to you. The second is its cost to your customers. The third is its resulting unit margin. The fourth value is external: the dollar value of the costs you can reduce in your customers' businesses or the dollar value of the new sales revenues you can help them attain with each product or system. These four sets of dollar values allow you to know if you are going to be able to meet the two major objectives of every key account sale. One is being certain that your customer will gain improved profit as a result of buying from you. The other is being certain that your own profit will be improved as a result of selling to your customer. If both profits can be improved by a sale, you have the basis for a key account penetration.

Your problem-solving products and their values represent the corollary of your information on your customer's problems and their values. On the surface, it may seem that the products on your side and the dollar values on the customer's side are being exchanged in a key account sale. But your data base will remind you that this is not the case. The actual exchange is a transfer of values: your customer's dollar values for your own dollar values. To say the same thing from a customer's point of view, a sale is a trade of a customer's current costs plus the added costs of doing business with you for your near-term and future improvement of customer profits.

Putting a Data Base to Work

Dresser-Wayne is a manufacturer and marketer of retail management control systems. One of its major lines of business is a single-source system supplied to gasoline retailer chains. It serves major oil company retail outlets and service stations, independent oil service stations, and convenience stores that also market gasoline. Its system consists of gas dispenser pumps, electronic control consoles that operate and monitor the pumps, automatic cash registers, automatic service equipment, and data storage and handling capabilities.

To the individual gas station retailer, the benefits of Dresser-Wayne's system are the timely profit reports on sales that provide the flexibility to change pricing quickly to correspond to peak and off-peak driving hours, accurate cost control, inventory control, and reduced labor. The system also safeguards against down time and can lower the costs of station design by saving space and increasing the throughput of customer traffic within the smaller space. The retailer's home office benefits too. It receives data faster and more accurately on sales and inventory. The data are more practical. They can be used to reduce costs and improve sales revenues by allowing improvements in the delivery schedules to each station. In addition, one supervisor at the head office can manage 12 stations instead of 6, thereby saving high-priced labor costs at the supervisor level of the chain.

The key account sales force of Dresser-Wayne is equipped with an APACHE type of data system. Each market segment—the major oil companies, the independents, and the convenience stores—has its individual data base. The general benefits that Dresser-Wayne can offer to all three segments are similar: improved profits through increased sales and reduced costs with greater security and control. But the specific benefits vary with the market segment and the problem to be solved. Accordingly, the APACHE data system is organized to allow each key account sales representative to answer questions like these:

1. Where is the problem at the station level? Is it principally an inventory control problem based on poor cash management? Is it a credit control problem? Are receipts and distribution at the heart of the problem? Or is it a question of labor skills or honesty, quality of maintenance, or the efficiency of present station design and the resulting efficiency of customer throughput?

2. Where is the problem at the home office level? Is it a problem of data control and reporting, cash management, or supervisory management?

3. Is this a product sales opportunity, a system-selling opportunity, or is there opportunity here for the sale of a superproduct composed of several gas pumps, monitoring consoles, a cash management control system, data storage and handling modems, and a training program?

4. Is this a lease or a buy opportunity?

5. Is there an opportunity to sell a plan to reconstruct individual gas stations to increase traffic, or is it more cost-effective to focus on improving station profit contribution from existing layouts?

6. What are the total costs to be reduced? What are the total sales revenues to be gained? What are the investment offsets required to achieve these results? What net profit will result to the customer and to us? What is the return on investment?

The APACHE data system reports on the total number of outlets that can be affected in each chain, identifies each one as being among the top 10 percent, in the middle, or among "all others," and specifies the average number of gallons it moves each month along with other products and services. Data are also included on each station manager's purchase preferences, workforce, and cost structure, and use of competitive equipment. Similar information is also available on home office managers.

Key account sales representatives at Dresser-Wayne consult with their decision-maker partner, the APACHE data system. The APACHE partner shares the type of customer information that is partially shown in Figures 9, 10, and 11. These three screens are devoted to the convenience store segment of Dresser-Wayne's market.

On the Problem/Opportunity Summary Screen in Figure 9, a sales representative has asked the APACHE partner to show the monthly dollar profit currently being contributed by key functions and characteristics of stores in the ABC Convenience Stores chain located in New York State. Some of these dollar values will be positive. Others will be negative contributions to profit. The positive values may indicate sales opportunities for

Figure 9.   Problem/opportunity summary screen.

Market Segment: Convenience stores
Customer: ABC Convenience Stores, Inc.
State/Region: New York/Northeast

	MONTHLY PROFIT CONTRIBUTION
OUTLET	
Credit control	$_____
Inventory control	_____
Cash control	_____
Staff productivity	_____
Maintenance	_____
Throughput efficiency	_____
Site layout/size	_____
HOME OFFICE	
Data control and report	_____
Cash management	_____
Supervisor productivity	_____
Communications	_____
Total contribution/Month	$_____
Total contribution/Year	$_____

Dresser-Wayne if they are lower than average. The negative values may indicate sales opportunities if they can be reduced or eliminated.

The APACHE proposal partner also tells the sales representative the contributions to profit being made by four functions at the chain's home office. These may provide supplementary sales opportunities.

If the business function of inventory control shows a negative profit contribution or only a small positive contribution to the chain's profit in Figure 9, it can be analyzed as a separate problem area on the screen shown in Figure 10. The problem of stock-out can be intensively evaluated according to its gallonage and dollar values. If

Figure 10.   Problem analysis screen.

Market Segment: Convenience stores
Customer: ABC Convenience Stores, Inc.
State/Region: New York/Northeast
Business Function: Inventory control
Problem: Stock-out

                                                                            ANALYSIS

Average time out of stock   _____

Number of times out of stock per year   _____

Average number of gallons pumped per hour   _____

Margin per gallon (¢)   _____

the sales representative believes these values can be improved, the APACHE system will create a proposal to compare improved benefits with the current situation. The APACHE proposal partner will then show Figure 11, pointing out the dollar benefits that the representative can bring to the customer on a weekly and monthly basis for any individual store or for the entire ABC chain.

When Dresser-Wayne sales representatives stand before their customers' top-tier decision makers, they hold in their hands a profit improvement proposal. Its "product" is new profits for the customer.

Figure 11.   Benefit analysis screen.

Market Segment: Convenience stores
Customer: ABC Convenience Stores, Inc.
State/Region: New York/Northeast
Business function: Inventory control

	BENEFITS	
	$ Monthly	$ Weekly
Product loss		
Leakage	_____	_____
Vapor	_____	_____
Theft	_____	_____
Stock-out	_____	_____
Carrying excess inventory	_____	_____

Dresser-Wayne used to sell ironware: gas pumps and related equipment. Then its strategy was to sell groups of products and services called systems: not just gas pumps, but control consoles, inventory gauges, automatic cash registers, and data modems with some training and a lease program. Now Dresser-Wayne has transcended products, equipment, and systems to sell improved customer profitability. It has moved from a "hardware" selling company that did business in iron to a "software" selling company that did business in data to a true retail management company that does business in helping its customers grow their own businesses.

Monitoring Against Penetration Plans

A customer data base can play a dual role in your key account management. As the proposal partner of your sales representatives, it can help improve your profit on sales by encouraging the presentation of optimal solutions to customer problems. In its second role, the data base can help you monitor the fulfillment of each sales representative's account penetration plans.

When a customer data base has been structured, it can be used to store your plans as well as customer problems and their solutions. Plans will still be prepared in the form of written documents. In addition, though, their major elements can be translated into easily accessible data. At any time, you can call up this data on your APACHE data base for a performance review across a wide range of major subjects:

1. You can compare the total planned revenues and profits that have been projected by all your penetration plans with actual performance on a monthly, quarterly, or random basis.

2. You can learn the contributions coming to you from each major industry you serve, to see whether you are on or off plan.

3. You can evaluate the performance of each key account representative or team.

4. You can analyze the acceptance of each major product, service, or system you sell according to each industry it is sold to, each customer that buys it, each account team that sells it, and each problem it solves.

From your performance reviews, you can get a head start on detecting new areas of opportunity that may be opening up faster than expected. You can detect trouble spots before they enlarge. You can alert your key account sales force to the most likely winning strategies as soon as they become hot and warn them away from product offerings and sales strategies that seem to be cooling down. You can apply coaching and counseling while you can still remedy a situation rather than with after-the-fact hindsight.

In addition to these day-to-day advantages, there are also longer-term benefits for you in your role as sales strategist. By progressively monitoring your achievement against plan, you can begin to assemble the success factors that you will see emerging from your reviews. You will notice the coincidental association of certain strategies with results. You will become aware of the heightened acceptance of certain products, services, or systems. You will recognize certain patterns of industry interest or the beginnings of trends. Based on these monitorings, you will be able to create your own personal guidelines to the two most crucial aspects of key account sales:

1. How to increase the speed of penetration, thereby condensing the time costs and operating costs of the sales cycle.

2. How to increase the depth of penetration into high-level decision positions, thereby expanding the number of authoritative information sources who can partner with you.

Applying Triage to Account Team Management

Applying the guidelines to accelerate your account penetration can be aided and abetted by managing your key teams according to the principle of "triage," or threeing. Under triage, each account team is grouped into one of three categories. Each category defines the primary strategy that the teams within it are using to make their penetrations.

The first triage category is composed of the "horizontals," who sell to the easiest customer opportunities. They cover a customer broadly, generating a large number of proposals that may get too involved with low-priority problem areas. A second category is the "verticals." They concentrate their proposals intensely on a relatively narrow range of customer opportunities. They may miss the big picture, letting additional problem areas go by the board that they could also solve.

The third category in the triage is the "diagonals." They are in trouble. As their name suggests, they need to be straightened out by replacement or restructuring.

Your management action with each account team is dictated by its category, as Figure 12 shows. The horizontals will benefit by having their priorities challenged: Are they the same as the customer's priorities? They will have to be taught to increase the depth of their penetration into priority areas rather than continue to be broad-scale surface skimmers.

The verticals, on the other hand, need to adopt a wider base of customer penetration: Are all major problems being covered? They will have to be taught to multiply their options by strengthening their penetration to include additional data sources and by analyzing their data for more clues.

Maintaining Account Continuity

Partnerships are dependent on continuity. When one of the partners changes, the partnership becomes at risk. If the customer partner is the one who is being changed, whether by promotion, transfer, or retirement, the effect may be the same as if the customer company itself were

Figure 12.   Triage management categories.

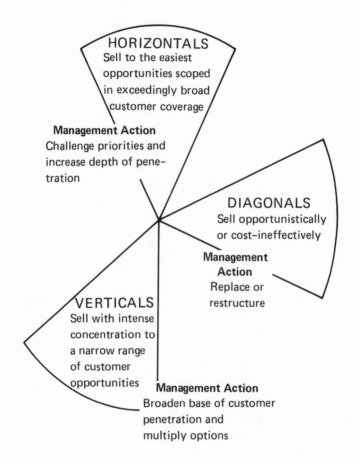

changing suppliers. If the sales representative partner is the one who changes, the customer may be open to considering a competitive partner, since a readjustment will be required in any case.

If your key account sales are operated from a customer data base, you may be able to reduce the loss of momentum or, at worst, the loss of an account, when one of your representatives moves up or out.

Over the years of a continuing customer relationship, where many changes may have taken place on both sides of an account, the seller's data base can be the sole source of continuity. It has a prodigious memory. It never forgets. And it is always ready to teach an account's problems, opportunities, and profit-improvement history to anyone who wants to learn.

Many key account customers take comfort in the knowledge that their profit-improving partner maintains a data base on the problems they have solved together, the business functions that have benefited, the systems that have delivered the benefits, and the contributions they have made to operating productivity and financial improvement. For many of the same reasons, supplier sales managers take comfort, too.

When you bring into your own business the ongoing knowledge of a customer's industry, the company as a whole, and the problems of the specific divisional functions you serve, you own an equity in your relationship with the customer. The equity is your ability to maintain a continuous stream of profit improvement proposals against the customer's operations, free from interruption. The uninterrupted flow of profits from your business is a vital resource. It is the equivalent of a line of credit. Without the certainty that the customer can get it when needed, the value it holds may evaporate. The axiom of prudent business management that undependable money is unspendable money can cause the customer to look elsewhere for a source of ongoing profit improvement.

Every new sales representative who moves onto a key account can be moved first through its data base for an automated briefing session. No one needs to take time out for training in the account's principal problems, opportunities, decision-maker propensities, or competitors. The briefing can be repeated as often as necessary or desired. Specific areas of inquiry can be studied intensively. Interrelationships in the data can be creatively cross-referenced.

The same advantages can be made available to new or newly promoted customer partners. They, too, can be briefed by your data base to equip them with an early awareness of the values their business has received from your partnership, the types of problems that have been solved together, and the opportunities that still remain on the mutual agenda contained in your account penetration plan.

Keeping Current on Customer Problems

A customer business is a collection of cost problems and revenue opportunities. Its costs eat away at its revenues. When one cost is reduced or eliminated, another cost is often revealed as the next candidate for cutback. At the same time, the search for new revenues incurs new costs. This creates the need to make sales revenue production more cost-effective. The cycle is endless.

At every point in the cycle of costs-revenues-costs, opportunity is created for the improvement of customer profit by helping to reduce costs and increase sales. This is the basis for key account penetration.

In this context, your sales representatives have twin missions with their customers. One is to penetrate the customer's dollar resources and come back with a maximum contribution by selling something. The other is to penetrate the customer's information resources and come back with a maximum contribution by learning something. What each representative learns will become another input for your data base.

Bringing back sales has been the traditional emphasis. Information has been supplementary, amassed informally and regarded as a bonus accompanying the sales transaction. In top-tier selling, however, information is a coequal objective with every sale. It is the raw material from which new sales will be proposed. Consequently, it is the source of your future profits.

A sale without information leading to subsequent sales is only half a transaction. An installation without developing knowledge of further problems to be solved is only half an installation. A proposal without insight into follow-on proposals is only half a proposal.

The existence of a customer data base provides a natural repository for attracting current information on a continually updated basis. It gives information a home, acting as a highly visible symbol of the sales representatives' companion responsibility. This responsibility can be integrated into their position descriptions so that standards for performance are met only when they have made customer data deposits of required value during each evaluation period.

Using your APACHE data base to maintain up-to-date knowledge of customer problems is an organized way to keep yourself "in the market." By allowing the data base to put pressure on you to certify that it is always up to date, you insure your involvement with customer businesses on a close, continuing basis—the best guarantee you can have of being accepted over time as your key accounts' preferred profit improver.

Marketing the Data Base

From the perspective of key account sales management, a customer data base is an investment in raising the profit contribution from major sales. Financially speaking, though, a data base represents a cost center. Its cost can frequently be unburdened—either in whole or in part—by the selective marketing of some of its contents.

In this way, a data base can become more than a contributor to improved profitability from key account sales. It can become a profit center itself, based on the sale of a new product in your line, called information.

One of the most significant characteristics of growth businesses in the period between 1980 and 2000 will be their ability to market a product line of "information" along with whatever other products and services they offer.

Data marketing can take one or both of two forms:

1. *Selling customer industry information.* Information from your data base on the industries of your key customer accounts is often marketable in periodic survey form to suppliers who are not competitive with you but who serve these same industries. Since this type of data is generally derived almost totally from public information, the value you can add to it as a reseller is principally in providing accessibility from a single source and customized packaging. A second market may exist within a customer industry itself, where its own member companies, associations, lenders, and investors may find confirmation or new insights in your knowledge of its trends, chief needs, key ratios, and future projections of volume and profits.

2. *Selling solution information.* The solutions for key account problems that you and your competitors sell represent marketing opportunities for many types of

other businesses that supply your ingredients, components, modules, and piece parts. Your solutions—
especially to the extent that they are on the leading edge
of technology—can be the market targets for myriads of
supplier businesses who need to know what they themselves must gear up to manufacture and sell. In many
industries, no formal source of this information exists on
an authentic basis. Formalizing its distribution through a
regular medium may provide a business opportunity that
can serve two purposes: It can bring in new profits and,
at the same time, help consolidate your position as the
premier problem solver in your customer industries.

Marketing the contents of your key account data
base can be done on a standardized or custom basis.
Newsletters, cassettes, seminars, reports, or magazines
can compose the media of standard distribution. Special
reports and chartered presentations can be customized to
meet more specific needs. Your marketing can be accomplished through mail distribution or electronic transfer
into other data bases, without intervention of a sales
force. Or you can organize a traditional sales staff to sell
direct to key accounts.

In addition to bringing in profits, being in the information business brings in a second benefit as well. Once
you become established as a supplier of data, information will flow to you as well as flow from you. The rich-
ness of your customer data base will grow, fortified by a
variety of inputs that will be directed to you precisely
because you are a recognized source.

Accessing Customer Information

Your customer data base should become a utility in
your key account operations, every bit as central and
continuingly useful to them as the other utilities of light,

heat and air conditioning, and power. Operationally, the central position of customer data in key account planning means that they are at the pivot point of all your penetration strategy making. Functionally, however, you have a choice. Access to the data themselves may be either centralized or distributed.

In some companies, the data base is centralized at their headquarters location. A corporate or divisional staff is trained to input new data, maintain currency and accuracy for the data base, and has sole access to it. Under this arrangement, key account sales representatives are responsible for banking regular deposits of customer information. The central staff, in turn, is responsible for processing requests for proposals from the sales force and delivering them to the sales representatives who have originated the requests. In many cases, a recommended proposal and an optional proposal will be created if an alternative penetration strategy is discovered or felt to be desirable as a standby.

When a customer data base is centralized in this manner, the guardian staff who control access to it become the sales representatives' proposal partners—or at least the human agents of the computerized APACHE data base partner.

This type of centralized organization of the customer data base offers several advantages. The permanent staff can become proficient in generating profit improvement proposals. As their skills increase with practice, their ability will also grow to perceive opportunities for standard solutions to recurrent business function problems, to cross-reference solutions from one proposal to another, and to suggest comprehensive supersystems that can solve complex customer problems. At times, the central staff may take on consultative roles in these areas.

Key customer decision makers can be invited to visit the central location to observe their data in the act of being updated or used in proposal generation. Industry sources can attend seminars based on trends and projections in their business segments. The data base can become a corporate data center. Architecturally and operationally, it can be made into the solar plexus of your marketing operations. In smaller scale, the same advantages can be located at regional subcenters.

Other companies make full-time allies of key account representatives and their data bases. Each representative is equipped with his or her own terminal, which can be portable or fixed at the representative's local office or at home. In this form of the "buddy system," the representative and his or her data base become the proposal partners that are "one and inseparable." Each representative is responsible for maintaining the accuracy and timeliness of customer information and for using it to create his or her own proposals.

Given personal access on a 24-hour-day, 7-day-week basis, a representative can be expected to develop an intense appreciation of the value of the data base and a high degree of intellectual curiosity in testing the feasibility of new solutions whenever they occur. Since the validity of the representative's proposals clearly depends on adherence to good maintenance procedures, it can generally be assumed that the data base will be well cared for. A small central staff can be made available to help each representative on a demand basis. Simultaneously, they can operate a headquarters installation for top management demonstration and corporate positioning purposes with top-tier customers and other influential constituencies.

Because key account selling is such a uniquely personal experience between a sales representative, customer decision makers, and the problem-solution information they develop together, there is no substitute for the decentralization of data base access to each representative. To the extent that key account representation can be personalized by each man or woman who sells— so that their customer is regarded as "my customer," their data base as "my proposal partner," and their proposals as "my proposals"—its success can be significantly enhanced.

Integrating Information and Operations

When you send your key account sales force out into the field, they represent your business to your major customers. Your key account data base represents your customers inside your own business. If you look at the role of your data base in this way, you will be able to see that it fulfills two prime functions:

1. In organization terms, it is the correlate of your sales force. It acts as the "Mr. Inside" of your customer representation.
2. In operating terms, it is the partner of your sales force. It acts as the "Answerman" of their proposal process.

There is no alternative to an APACHE-type customer data base in either of these functions. Nothing else can represent your key accounts so well inside your business. Nothing else can partner so well with your sales force to generate penetration proposals.

In sales management, it is traditional to compare all investment options against the criterion of being able to afford "one more sales representative." In many cases—

perhaps most—it might be better to hire the additional representative rather than spend a similar amount of money on something else. There is one exception: if the option can multiply the effectiveness of your present sales force so that you gain the equivalent of additional representatives without having to hire, train, or compensate them. An APACHE data base is exactly such a multiplier. For the cost of somewhere between one and two key account representatives, including their total indirect expense allocations and support service burdens, your customer data base can make each of your existing representatives up to several hundredfold more productive.

How can this be so?

Your sales representatives who are equipped with customer information will sell from their information, not from a price list or product catalog.

They will sell the knowledge of their own business—solution knowledge—in a way that matches their knowledge of the problems in their customer businesses.

They will sell in customer language, which is the language of the financial and operating aspects of customer business functions. Top-tier customer managers speak this language, and they will share it with representatives who speak it also.

They will sell against customer problems, not against competitors who offer parity products at parity prices. They will defeat their competitors by the superior values of their financial and operating solutions, not on the basis of reduced price. As their values become accepted as the industry standards, the effects of competition on their sales will diminish.

They will sell to customer representatives who want to be sold, because they want their problems solved in the most profitable manner. Instead of defending against buying, they will help your representatives sell, because it is in their own self-interest to contribute as much as they can to their company's profit improvement.

No one or two additional sales representatives you may hire can have these effects on your current key account sales force.

Any newly hired representatives would be transient. They could leave, receive promotions, or be transferred. Your customer data base is permanent. It is an appreciating asset that becomes more valuable over time in the roles of your "Mr. Inside" of customer representation and the "Answerman" for your preparation proposals. It is always under your control, always accessible, and will never end up working for a competitor.

As the utilitarian nature of customer data bases becomes accepted as basic key sales management practice, it will become part of the one-two punch of key account penetration. Top managers in supplier companies will insist that their key account sales functions be data-based. Recruits will want to test a prospective employer's data base before hiring on. Key account representatives will leave one job for another in order to be supported by a superior data base. Key customers will insist that their major suppliers sell to them based on business function knowledge of their operations so that their profits may be optimally improved.

As key account data basing becomes commonplace, a customer data base will be the No. 2 element in the one-two penetration punch. The No. 1 element will always be the key account representative—the leader of the sales representative-data base team. It will be the representative's skill that will add the unique marginal values to the data base to endow it with superior usefulness.

A representative can embellish a data base with competitive values in several ways:

1. By taking care to stock it regularly, keep it up to date, and cross-reference its inputs in varied ways so that they can be integrated into many different types of inquiry.

2. By acting ingeniously to test and retest solutions to make certain they are creative, cost-effective, and comprehensive. When the crunch comes in neck-and-neck competitive showdowns, the order will go to the most creative solution: the one that creates the greatest profit for the customer.

3. By searching out the common denominators in successful penetration proposals, recording them in the data base in relation to the problems they apply to, and using them as standard frames of reference for future proposals. In many companies, as many as 80 percent of the components of successful solutions are repetitive.

4. By motivating customer decision makers to become involved with the representative as third partners in the data-base partnership, so that they can participate in updating its information, adding to it, and developing trust in the representative's penetration proposals.

5. By using data base information to counsel with customers on ways to improve their profit even though no opportunity for a sale is in prospect. The periodic gift of something of value without the expectation of compensation is a hallmark of the superior consultative sales representative.

In ways like these, the power of an APACHE data base can be fully harnessed as a key account sales tool, not just on the merits of its own intrinsic qualities, but supplemented with values added by the person it adds the most to—your key account sales representative.

6

Account Penetration Planning

How to Maximize Customer Contribution

Your key customer accounts are your single most precious resource. Nothing rivals their importance. They are your major source of profits. They are the major source of needs to which your technology, your product development and engineering, your manufacturing, and your marketing must respond. They are, in short, your core market.

Each key account is vital as a profit contributor. Opportunities you fail to serve in a key account are the most unaffordable losses you can suffer. The loss may be in more than profit. The entire account may be lost if a competitor can serve it better. On a short-term basis, the loss of a major customer is irreplaceable. In some industries where it may take five years or more to get back in the ball game, any loss becomes long-term. Meanwhile, all the potential upgrading and migration sales that could have flowed from your original penetration are forsaken as well.

The defection of a key customer, or the abdication

on your part of the opportunity to serve a key customer more comprehensively, is unsupportable. You should therefore treat every key account as if it were a market unto itself. You should analyze its problems and opportunities, quantify its contribution to you and your contribution to it through the sales of your solutions, and position yourself as one of its most significant profit improvers through a separate key account penetration plan.

A penetration plan is your annual blueprint for getting into and staying in the business of a principal customer. The way you get in is by improving the customer's profit. The way you stay in is by continuing the customer's profit improvement, extending it to the solution of new problems, and never letting go. Last year's profit improver who has let go is last year's supplier of choice.

The account penetration planning process requires you to answer the three critical questions that can determine up to 80 percent of your profitability on sales:

1. Who is my customer?
2. What can I do to improve my customer's profit?
3. What will my customer do for me in return?

The answer to the first question is crucial. Your customer is never a customer company as a whole, nor is it a customer division. It is a specific business function manager within a division whose costs you can reduce or whose contribution to sales you can increase. If you are IBM, your customer is not PepsiCo. Nor is it PepsiCo's Frito-Lay division. It is the manager of Frito-Lay's inventory control function, for example, whose profit contribution you will be improving.

Similarly, if you are AT&T, your customer is not Merrill Lynch or, within it, the Diversified Financial Services division. Nor is it the division's real estate management functions. Your penetration plan would be directed to the division. But the business function manager in real estate telemarketing is your customer. It is the manager's profit contribution you will be improving. If you are Nabisco, your customer is not Grand Union supermarkets. It is the dry cereal department management group throughout the chain.

Planning to penetrate business functions within divisions or departments of customer companies is a far cry from vending commodity merchandise to purchasing managers on a price-performance basis. It is a totally different business that is conducted on a tier of its own. It must be sold in a different manner. It must be planned in its own way to support the differences in sales strategy that a consultative approach demands.

Planning High Penetration Objectives

Key account penetration planning hinges on one central concept: maximizing contribution. Two kinds of contribution are involved. One is your profit contribution to a customer. You must maximize it. The other is a customer's profit contribution to you. You must maximize it also. This defines your prime objective in key account penetration. You will have to be a maximizer of profits.

To be a profit maximizer is a different role than acting as a need analyst or a benefit provider or a problem solver. All of these are intermediary steps. The ultimate step is that through needs analysis, the provision of benefits, and the solving of problems, profits become improved. Unless this takes place, all the intermediate objectives will be in vain.

High penetration objectives—objectives for your

customer's top tier and for you as well—are financial objectives. Nothing supersedes them. They must come first in your penetration plan, because they are the purpose of the plan. The only reason to plan is to be able to set and achieve high financial objectives.

Your plan's objectives should be stated in the following manner:

1. The most likely profit contribution that will be made *by us* to the customer:
   1.1   This year
   1.2   Next year
   1.3   Third year
2. The most likely profit contribution that will be made *to us* by the customer:
   2.1   This year
   2.2   Next year
   2.3   Third year

"Most likely" profits are a conservative, slightly to the left of the middle of the road estimate. They are a trifle more bullish than bearish, but only a trifle. They represent the contributions that can be expected if most strategies work according to plan, and if there are no important hitches that have not been planned for. In practice, they should come out just about right.

If you help customers improve their profits from incremental sales, you will have to adjust the gross profits they make before taxes by the customers' effective tax rate before you commit to an objective. If you improve customer profits by saving or eliminating costs that can flow directly to the bottom line, you can calculate their profits as net incremental gain. Only the net counts. Neither you nor your customers can take anything else to the bank and draw dollar for dollar from it.

The total gross contribution you expect to make to

your customers will be the sum of all the profit improvement proposals you plan to have reach fulfillment
or partial fulfillment in their business functions during the
year. The contribution you plan for your customers to
make to you will be the sum of your profits from the sale
of each proposal that are collectible during the same
year. To help keep track of how effectively your key
account teams are managing the allocation of their resources to obtain each customer's contribution, you may
want to maintain two ratios. One compares profits to the
expenditures required to achieve them. This is a form of
return on investment. The second is the more traditional
ratio of your revenues to expenses.

Planning a High-Penetration Strategy Mix

Objectives are a plan's purpose. Strategies are the
plan's methods of achieving its purpose. In consultative
selling for key account penetration, a plan's strategies
are contained in its accompanying profit improvement
proposals. Each proposal represents a strategy to improve customer profit by solving a cost or sales problem.
If the customer is a not-for-profit organization, a government agency or department, your proposal strategies will
have to reduce costs and improve the dollar value of
productivity. Either way, your mix of strategies will need
to make a measurable impact on customer profit or operational performance or both.

Profit improvement proposals are the delivery vehicles for your penetration strategies. They are designed to
penetrate the customer's business at high-level points of
entry. Each proposal contains a strategy for solving a
specific customer problem. The strategy will be composed of a package of your products and services called a

system. All your proposals taken together for the period of a year constitute your annual strategy mix for a customer. There are three steps to take before you propose profit improvement.

ANALYZING A CUSTOMER'S BUSINESS POSITION

Every customer division whose functions you affect occupies a position on the life-cycle curve. If you define that position, understand its implications for your penetration strategy, and structure your profit improvement proposals in accord with it, you can significantly add to their hit ratio.

There are three customer business positions that have a determining effect on your strategy mix. They are the growth position, the stable position, and the position of decline. Each one presents a different penetration challenge.

1. *Penetrating a growth customer.* A growth customer is sales-driven. If you want to affect the sales function, you must increase its productivity so that it will be able to generate more profits per sale or to yield added profits from incremental sales. If you cannot affect sales, but instead, your impact on a customer's business is to reduce costs, the saving you achieve for the customer can be applied to support more sales. Your entire penetration strategy must focus on improving the customer's profit by increasing sales.

2. *Penetrating a stable customer.* A stable customer is driven from two directions at once. Sales must be increased, but not if it requires increased costs. If projected sales fail to result, the customer's stability can be threatened. Costs must be reduced, but not if it will reduce sales or market share. If sales fall, the customer's stability can be threatened. Your penetration strategy

can focus on improving profit through sales increases or cost decreases, but it must avoid the risk of increasing costs or decreasing sales in the process.

3. *Penetrating a declining customer.* A declining customer is cost-driven. If you can help it lower or eliminate a cost, you can often help improve profit on a dollar-for-dollar basis. The dollars the customer needs to slow the loss of market position will mostly have to come from funds reclaimed from costs. They are unlikely to be appropriated by management. As a result, your penetration strategy must focus on making the customer's cost structure relinquish money for use in running the business.

POSITIONING YOUR PENETRATION STRATEGIES

The purpose of analyzing a customer's business position is to be able to custom-tailor your penetration. If a customer is in a growth position, you must present yourself as an improver of profit on sales. If the customer is stable, you must present yourself as a profit improver by increasing sales or profits per sale on the one hand and, on the other, by decreasing costs. For a declining customer, you must present youself as being a profit improver through cost reduction.

Unless your position coincides with the customer's, you will never be able to create a partnership in profit improvement. The customer will not understand where you are coming from in your proposals. You, in turn, lacking a sense of your customer's objectives, will not know where the customer is going. As two unknowns, you will be talking past each other; you will be proposing to yourself.

To insure that your positioning is in gear with how your customer is positioned, your penetration strategy should be preceded by a positioning statement. The statement ought to contain three references: your position with reference to the customer, the customer's position on the life-cycle curve, and the general strategic direction you will adopt. A model statement reads as follows:

"In our penetration of the manufacturing functions of the ABC Company's XYZ Division, a stable business since 1982, we will position ourselves as the manufacturing vice-president's partner in profit improvement primarily by means of the reductions in cost we can deliver through our quality control system. We will also show how enhanced product quality can help improve profit through incremental sales."

Pinpointing Penetration Opportunities

A customer's inability to bring down a cost or the customer's need to increase profitable sales volume are major business problems. Accordingly, they may be your penetration opportunities. In order to find out, you will have to identify them and then put dollar values on them and on the most cost-effective solutions you can devise to counteract them. This is the information that should be loaded into your key account data system. Your sales representatives and their computerized APACHE proposal partner will use it to develop their profit improvement proposals.

Opportunities to penetrate a key account have a special genesis. A penetration opportunity does not automatically come into being simply because a customer has a problem and you happen to have a solution for it. Discovery is not opportunity. A penetration opportunity is determined by an analysis of three values:

1. *The dollar value of the customer's problem.* How significant is it? Is it making a significant negative contri-

bution to customer profit? Does it justify a significant expenditure for solution?

2. *The dollar values of the profits from your solution* that will accrue both to you and to the customer. How significant are they? When will they begin to flow? How long before their total amount finally accrues?

3. *The dollar values of the costs of your solution* that will be incurred both by you and by the customer. How significant are they? Are they all up-front or can some of them be paid for out of the solution's improved profits?

Penetration opportunities are entry points. You should regard them as windows. An opportunity window may be said to open when the following conditions can be met:

1. The dollar values of the profits from your solution exceed the dollar value of the customer's problem.
2. The dollar values of the profits from your solution exceed the dollar values of the costs of your solution.
3. The dollar values of the profits from your solution exceed the dollar values of the profits from competitive solutions.

The first condition insures that a customer problem is worth solving; that is, it is beneficial to solve. The second condition insures that a problem is profitable to solve. The third condition insures that your solution will be the preferred solution. All three conditions place the burden of proof squarely where it belongs—on the ability of your key account sales teams to create the most profitable solutions to customer problems in the business functions you can affect. This is the supreme standard of performance that can be devised for key account selling.

Proposing Profit Improvement

Profit improvement proposals are your basic sales tools for key account penetration. They are designed to permit you to penetrate at high customer levels and to sell at high-profit margins. Frequently they are tailored for specific high-level decision makers to reflect their functional or personal perspective on the customer problem you are proposing to solve. In all cases, they identify you as being in a service business that affects the financial state of the customer's business—the fundamental consultative positioning for key account penetration. There are three types of profit improvement proposals:

Entry proposals. When you penetrate a customer's business for the first time, or penetrate a new business function within the same customer account, you should construct a proposal that will guarantee your successful entry. First proposals must deliver. For this reason, they should be exceedingly conservative in the amounts of improved profit they promise and in the time frames they allow for its inflow. A safe rule is to "promise less profit and allow more time." Showing speedy results is the paramount consideration, demonstrating to the customer that profit can be improved and doing so in the shortest possible time. This dictates that you should select an entry problem whose scope you can limit and whose forthcoming solution you can vouch for at the highest level of confidence.

Mainstay proposals. Your core strategies for customer penetration are the mainstays of your annual plan. These are your bread-and-butter proposals that are designed to solve comprehensive customer problems and deliver major amounts of profits to both of you as their reward. As a group, they should yield about 80 percent of your annual profit contribution to each account and a similar proportion of each account's contributions to you. When this occurs, you will know that you are managing your key accounts "according to plan."

Opportunity proposals. No matter how well you plan, opportunities will rise up in the course of your progressive penetration of each customer. The solution of one problem almost always reveals another. The success of one solution almost always provokes interest in another application somewhere else.

As your customer data base grows, more opportunities for you to propose will become available. Even though you have not planned them, you should keep on your toes for the chance occurrences that invite a proposal. When they come, you can structure a solution for them. Some of these opportunities will be entry proposals. Others can turn into mainstay proposals that open up entire new areas of profitability for you and your customers.

All three types of proposing need to take into consideration four guidelines: following the proper sequence for the proposal, justifying high margins, partnering with top-tier decision makers to implement the proposal, and migrating initial sales success.

Sequencing the Proposal

A profit improvement proposal follows a logical sequence. It begins with a definition of the operating and financial aspects of the customer problem you are proposing to solve. From there, it defines your solution in terms of its operating and financial benefits. It then specifies the dollar differences between the solution and

the problem. This is the profit that will bring improvement to the customer's current situation.

The proposal's purpose is to move your goods. Yet
as much as 90 percent of its content will regularly be
devoted to information about what you can do financially
for a customer's business rather than what your products
and services can do in terms of performance benefits.

Of all this information, another 90 percent will be
composed of business function operating information
that the customer already knows and that you must
know, too, in order to help improve profiit. These facts
must have a permanent home. There is no better place
for them than your key account data base.

A profit improvement proposal is solution-driven,
problem-oriented, and profit-centered. Customer problems must be presented in the context of their effect on
profits. Your solutions must be presented in the same
context.

Vendor proposals are based on competitive claims
supported by specifications. Consultative proposals are
contrasts between two types of information: what a customer's managers know about their own business, and
what you know about bringing improved profit to it.
Competitive   comparisons   are   totally   absent.
Specifications of products, services, or systems go into
an appendix at the rear.

JUSTIFYING HIGH MARGINS

The dollar value of the cost incurred by a customer
to obtain your solution is your price. If you were selling
to a customer's bottom tier in the manner of a vendor,
your price would be based on a resolution of your costs
and fair market value—the prices being charged by your

major competitors. This would guarantee you low margins.

The end objective of consultative selling is to obtain high margins. To do so, you must free price from cost and competitive pricing points. The dollar value that a key account customer pays will be higher than vendor prices only if you base them on the profit dollars that your proposal calculates will be generated by your solution. The greater the extent to which you improve customer profit, the greater justification you can have for demanding a high-margin price.

Consultative pricing is value-based pricing. The value it is based on is the dollar value of customer profits that are derived from your solution. Your incentive to supply high amounts of improved profits to your key accounts is built into your pricing policy. In this way, your individual objectives come together as one. You both want the highest possible profits to accrue to the customer. Added profit dollars are essential to capitalize business growth. The customer must have improved profits in order to justify paying your margins and to provide the incentive to buy from you again.

Unlike vendor selling, where price is the central haggling point—the customer wants the lowest price, while the vendor wants the highest—profits are the issue in consultative sales. Both parties want them to be high. With this powerful mutual objective at the heart of your consultative relationships, a natural incentive exists on both sides to form close continuing partnerships.

PARTNERING WITH TOP-TIER DECISION MAKERS

Vendors and their customers enjoy adversary relationships. Vendors "overcome customer objections," say "yes . . . but" a lot, and routinely force trial closes on customers who, at the same time, are defending themselves with equal artifice and guile. Consultative selling relationships are very different. The sellers learn as much as they can about customer business problems that they can affect, study their contribution to customer profit, and propose how they can improve the contribution. Since their customers spend their working days doing the exact same things, consultative sellers and their customers work in parallel instead of on a collision course.

People who work in parallel can work as partners. Selling partners play consultative roles. Buying partners become clients. Clients are not just customers with feathers. They are customers who share common objectives with their consultants. As a result of sharing objectives, there is no "yours" or "mine." A single set of purposes is blended. Both partners are dedicated to the partnership because neither can benefit his or her needs as well in any other way. The key word between partners becomes "we."

Partners conduct their business in distinctive ways. They provide easy access to each other, no matter how high their levels or what their disparities may be. They share information with each other. Principally, the information is about the customer's business, because no profit improvement is possible without a data base of problems and penetration opportunities. They exchange speculation about solutions to problems in the customer's business in a manner that is free from the pressure of early commitment or self-seving foreclosure of the dialog, even on a trial-close basis. Once they achieve results together, they tend to shut out competitors for each other's time, information, and resources.

From a customer's point of view, your key account sales representative and support team serve as dedicated resources that are knowledgeable about a customer's profit situation and capable of improving it. From your key account representative's point of view, customers are dedicated resources, too. Customers provide knowledge of prime penetration opportunities. They provide the counsel of their decision makers and their influencers on a confidential basis, further revealing their business needs. They provide profitable sales and potentially endless migrations of initial sales into fresh areas of implementation.

MIGRATING INITIAL SALES

Key account penetration through consultative selling is a reciprocal process. Preliminary partnering makes possible initial entry at top-tier levels. Once entry has been accomplished, partnering should proceed apace so that migration opportunities open up beyond the initial sale. The purpose of preliminary partnering is to gain entry. The purpose of entry is to migrate, to penetrate a customer business in breadth and depth.

In addition to the obvious benefit of providing you with ongoing high-margin sales opportunities, migration offers several other advantages. It helps amortize the cost of your original penetration investments for sales team training and data collection. It helps develop new information sources about a customer business. It spreads awareness of your consultative positioning. And it helps you deny opportunistic chances for your competitors to move in on a problem that you can, and should, solve.

Some migrations occur naturally. The solution of one problem leads progressively to the discovery of another. Or a solution in one division of a customer business stimulates internal interest about its transfer to a similar functional problem in another division. Other migrations will take place only as a result of effort. You will have to search out opportunities in the nooks and crannies of your customer businesses, relying on your partners to coach you about the most productive areas to explore and to point out the most cooperative guides to ask for advice.

The objective of penetrating a customer business in depth is to serve all major needs with your major products, services, or systems. This concept can be called maximizing "share of customer" as long as it is understood that it is not simply a volume criterion—it is a standard of the importance of your involvement. If you are significantly involved, you can become the preferred supplier of major offerings for your customers' major needs. Penetration in depth is inextricably tied to penetration in important areas of a business. Migration must be a selective policy whose aim is to consolidate your position as profit improver of the most vital functions you can affect.

The ideal migration timetable builds improving profit in one function as the jumping-off place for the next one. In this way, you can extract maximum learning value from each experience. You can also avoid stretching your resources too thin across more assignments than you can handle. It pays to remember that migration works both ways. One significant success encourages permission to try another. One significant failure discourages permission to try anything more at all.

Optimizing the Customer's Mix

Before a key customer becomes a partner, and you are still faced with the problem of making your initial penetration, your choice of entry strategy can be critical.

It can determine your rate of penetration, the perceived professionalism of your claim of consultative positioning, and in many cases, whether or not you penetrate at all. By thinking of the customer's current way of managing a business function as consisting of a "mix" of various suppliers' products and services and then offering to optimize the mix—that is, help it deliver its optimal contribution to profit—you may be able to make penetration when all other strategies will be rebuffed.

Every customer has allocated certain resources to each function. Some of these resources are supplied internally. They consist of the customer's own people and the processes they perform. The remaining resources come from outside. They consist of products, services, and systems that have been purchased from a variety of suppliers. Taken together, these internal and externally obtained resources are the customer's current operating "mix." If you want to penetrate it, you will have to improve the ability of the mix to contribute higher profits or greater productivity. There are three ways you can accomplish this objective:

1. You can supplant one or more elements in the current mix. If the mix is labor-intensive, you may be able to reduce its cost by substituting an automated process or eliminating an operation altogether. Or you may be able to combine multiple processes in a customer's sales function, such as forecasting and inventory control, eliminating overlapping or duplicated costs.

2. You can substitute your product or process for a competitive product or process that is part of the current mix. The basis for your recommendation must be that improved financial benefits will accrue to the customer if the mix is altered—not simply that more advantageous performance benefits will be realized.

3. You can restructure the mix in such a significant

manner that you will be the sole knowledgeable expert in its revamped composition, operation, and contribution to improved profits. Your identification as the sole source, or at least the originating source, of a new functional approach can help pull through your penetration as well as make it easier to push. In addition to the improvement in profits from becoming your customer, the prestige of working with the industry innovator will provide an extra motivation for customers to become partners with you.

The specific tactics of penetrating by means of optimizing a customer's mix will depend on the industry you serve.

If you sell personal care products to major supermarket and drug chains, you can penetrate by optimizing the mix of their current displays in terms of the number of facings they allocate to your products and competitors', the location of your facings, and the type of displays. The proof of your optimization will have to be quantified in financial and operating benefits, such as profit improvement per square or linear foot, overall improvement from the personal care department contribution per store, or improved profit contribution from related-item sales.

If you sell financial services like stocks and bonds, insurance, real estate investments, or money market funds to affluent individuals, you can penetrate by optimizing the mix of their current portfolios in terms of growth potential, risk, and current payout. The proof of your optimization will have to be quantified in dollar benefits such as higher earnings, lowered taxes, or increased net worth.

Figures 13 through 17 show how a sales representative who sells scientific instruments can work with an APACHE proposal partner to help optimize the mix of a key account laboratory customer.

Figure 13.   Equipment configuration analysis: present mix.

	Number per Year	Price	Annual Cost
Equipment			
Instrument A	_____	_____	_____
Instrument B	_____	_____	_____
Instrument C	_____	_____	_____
Instrument D	_____	_____	_____
Accessory Sets			
Set 1	_____	_____	_____
Set 2	_____	_____	_____
Set 3	_____	_____	_____
Set 4	_____	_____	_____
Materials			
Material XX	_____	_____	_____
Material YY	_____	_____	_____
Material ZZ	_____	_____	_____

In Figures 13 and 14, the sales representative has asked the APACHE partner to reach into its data base and show the customer's current equipment configuration. The mix includes instruments and their accessory sets and materials that are consumed by the instruments. The APACHE partner then shows the representative the financial costs that the customer incurs from the present mix. Four categories of cost contribution are shown in Figure 14. The two figures taken together give the representative a bird's-eye view of the

Figure 14.   Financial analysis: present mix.

DEPRECIATION
   Total annual instrument depreciation $_____
   (Total # instruments × average price/useful life)

LEASE COST
   Total annual instrument lease cost $_____
   (Total # leased instruments × average lease cost/month × 12)

MAINTENANCE
   Total annual instrument maintenance cost $_____
   (Total # leased instruments × total # purchased instruments × average annual maintenance cost)

INTEREST ON PURCHASE PRICE
   (Total # instruments purchased × average purchase price × cost of Money/100)

---

customer's laboratory function in terms of its hardware and software components and their costs. The sales representative's challenge is clear: Can the customer do better?

In Figure 15, the representative's APACHE partner shows a more optimal mix of equipment for the customer. According to the financial analysis of this mix in Figure 16, the representative will learn if fewer categories of instruments and accessory sets can achieve savings for the customer over and above the costs of the present mix. If so, the APACHE partner will create the Net Benefit Analysis shown in Figure 17, which will become the focal point of the representative's profit improvement proposal.

All customer businesses operate through mixes in their major functions. Some mixes are simply conglomerations of products. Others contain services such as training or maintenance. Others are composed of systems that, in turn, are composed of subsystems. You will have

*Figure 15.   Equipment configuration analysis: optimal
           mix.*

	Number per Year	Price	Annual Cost
Equipment			
Instrument A–B	_____	_____	_____
Instrument C	_____	_____	_____
Accessory Sets			
Set 1–2	_____	_____	_____
Set 3	_____	_____	_____
Materials			
Material XX	_____	_____	_____
Material YY	_____	_____	_____

Figure 16.   Financial analysis: optimal mix.

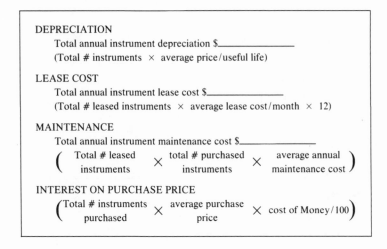

DEPRECIATION
    Total annual instrument depreciation $_____
    (Total # instruments × average price/useful life)

LEASE COST
    Total annual instrument lease cost $_____
    (Total # leased instruments × average lease cost/month × 12)

MAINTENANCE
    Total annual instrument maintenance cost $_____
    (Total # leased instruments × total # purchased instruments × average annual maintenance cost)

INTEREST ON PURCHASE PRICE
    (Total # instruments purchased × average purchase price × cost of Money/100)

to determine the mix into which you fit, what you can contribute to it in "hardware" and "software," and what dollar values of improvement you can propose. The mix becomes your market. It is where you fit, where you operate, and where you belong. Even more, it must be-

Figure 17.   Net benefit analysis: optimal mix.

	Optimal Mix	Present Mix
Expenses		
Depreciation	_____	_____
Equipment write-off	_____	_____
Lease cost	_____	_____
Maintenance	_____	_____
Interest on purchase price	_____	_____
Materials	_____	_____
Labor	_____	_____
Freight	_____	_____
Total Expense	_____	_____
BENEFITS		
Investment tax credit	_____	_____
Trade-in	_____	_____
Risk management	_____	_____
Financial risk reduction (opportunity cost)	_____	_____
Instrument standardization	_____	_____
Total Benefits	_____	_____
Net Expense	_____	_____
Net Benefit	_____	_____
Net Financial Benefit	_____	_____

come the area of your expertise. You must know how to make it produce profits in the most cost-effective manner. You must know this better than anyone else. You must master the operation of the mix so well that you can present yourself to your customers as their industry's "mixmaster."

Customer mixes usually lag behind the optimal mix. They frequently represent a sizable investment. They also are tied to a customer's learning curve. Customer people have learned how to operate their current mix. They have become familiar with its capabilities and its quirks. Training programs have been built around it. Cost and production schedules are established for it. Psychologically, it has become "the way we do things around here." For all these reasons, a current mix is hard to change, even with the promise of making it more optimal.

Penetration with a changed mix can only be made if there is a reason more powerful than all the reasons not to change, and if the problems of change can be made minimal. Improved productivity and profits are transcendent reasons to change. They are, to play on words, bottom-line reasons. They have more meaning than appeals to "be first," "be modern," "be competitive," or "be positioned for the future." The appeal that can win must be the appeal to "be more profitable now."

Customers know how easily improved profits can be consumed by the price of change, even for an admittedly more optimal mix. Your key account sales teams will have to surround their financial benefits with supplementary benefit values. First, they must provide a training program to teach the customer's people how to obtain the full financial benefits of their new mix. Second, they must provide service, maintenance, and a repair, replacement, and restocking program so that the operation of the new mix can be continuous and all but minor down-time averted. Third, they must be supported by a broad base of industry data on the performance and profitability characteristics of the mix they propose. This will help them be perceived as working from a credible source, have ready answers to customer questions, and act as true students of what they sell as well as professional instructors in the field of its profit contribution.

Making Penetration Plans Tangible

Key account penetration must be prepared as written documents. They should set down your positioning with each account, your penetration objectives for improved profits to go to both you and your customers, the penetration strategy mix that will achieve your objectives in the most cost-effective way, the profit improvement proposals that will act as vehicles for your strategies, the control procedures you will apply on each account to make certain that the improvements in profit are being delivered on time, and the essential elements of information about the customer's business required to document the plan's strategic approach.

Each penetration plan should be ratified by its customer. When it has been accepted, it should be entered into your key account data base for permanent reference. Your present sales representative can have repeated access to it, as can your support teams. Other representatives can study it, incorporating some of its strategies where they may be relevant to their own accounts. Newly promoted sales representatives can bring themselves quickly up-to-date on their accounts by studying the planning that has preceded them, and that they must henceforth carry forward.

At the sales management level, the full roster of all penetration plans will be available for scanning. No matter how many key accounts you supervise, you will be able to call up their plans to help you manage them better, to monitor progress, to troubleshoot in advance of major problems, as well as to detect new opportunities before they can be seized by competitors.

Every year's plan for each customer will be an extension of its predecessors, carrying forward the progressive penetration of the account's business. Laid end-to-end, the plans will dovetail. Yet they will show significant change. Reviewing this change will be an educational experience for you and your long-term sales representatives—and for your customers. Your ability to improve their profit will increase. Your ability to define problems to solve and to specify solutions for them will sharpen. The creativity and timeliness of your solutions will be enhanced. Your knowledge of each customer's business will expand.

Auditing Delivery of the Benefits

You should audit on at least a semiannual basis the actual penetration against plan being made by each key account sales team or individual sales representative. Your audit should focus on three areas of diagnosis:

1. Are the prime sales opportunities within each key customer's business being addressed?
2. What is our hit ratio, the percentage of accepted proposals to those that have not been acted on in our favor?
3. Are we neglecting any prime sales opportunities that competitors can use to gain footholds into a key customer's business?

As a result of your answers to these questions, you will know how to manage each key account team. In most cases, coaching and counseling will suffice. Remedial training may also be needed. In more extreme cases, people may have to be reallocated.

Using the penetration-planning process as your guide, you will be able to evaluate each key account sales team according to the single most important criterion controlling its performance: How much customer opportunity is the team converting into incremental profit contribution?

Table 1 shows a summary form for visualizing each sales team's contribution. For each key account, it

Table 1. Key account contribution summary.

	TOTAL BILLED REVENUES	NET INCREMENTAL BILLED REVENUES	
ACCOUNT	($)	($)	(%)
A	16.5	2.0	13.1
B	16.9	2.2	14.9
C	7.5	0.5	14.6
D	9.2	0.7	15.6
E	6.2	0.1	16.7

itemizes the total billed revenues that act as the gross sum from which your net incremental revenues are derived. The form tells you at a glance the net increments in the form of dollars earned and as a percentage of expenses incurred to achieve them.

The companion figures will take you behind the numbers of the Key Account Contribution Summary. Figure 18 will reveal the sales opportunities that are being realized across all key accounts. You will be able to

Figure 18. Sales opportunities across accounts.

SOLUTION	CUSTOMER PROBLEM/OPPORTUNITY	ACCOUNT				
		A	B	C	D	E

determine how aggressively your principal solutions are being sold to benefit the major problems and opportunities of your key accounts. You will also learn how many accounts have similar problems that can be solved with the same solutions—or, if you sense an incongruity, explore why the same solution is being applied in such a broad-brush manner.

The third step in your audit is illustrated by Figure 19. On an individual account-by-account basis, you can analyze the profit contribution you are making to each key customer and the profit it is contributing to you from each problem you are solving in each divisional function you have penetrated. You can also remind yourself and your sales team of the major competition for the right to solve each problem whose solution you have not yet sold or proposed.

Partnering the Penetration-Planning Process

As a rule, vendors plan in private against the magic moment when they will propose—a moment in which they reveal for the first time their price-performance benefits. Then, having proposed, they wait for the customer to dispose. In consultative selling, the penetration plan is developed in partnership with the customer. You must take the initiative in preparing the plan. But you must invite the customer's participation in finalizing it.

The profit improvement proposals in an account penetration plan may represent major time, dollar, and human resource investments by a customer. The improved profits you will make available can represent significant incremental funds. You must acknowledge your customer's involvements. The penetration plan cannot be your plan alone. It cannot be your plan *for* a

Figure 19. Sales opportunities within accounts.

Customer Division / Function	Problem / Opportunity	Solution Sold (date) Proposed (date) To be proposed (date)	Competition	Profit	
				To Customer	To Us

customer. To be successful, it can only be a plan made jointly *with* the customer in your mutual best interests.

Each annual plan should be an amalgam of your awareness of a customer's prime needs and the customer's own awarenesses. Before your sales teams present their proposals, they should meet with their customers' top-and bottom-tier decision makers to gain agreement on the nature and scope of the problems you have elected to solve. At the same time, they should obtain customer reaction to the profit-improvement solutions they have decided to propose. A revised target list of problems may come out of these discussions. These will be jointly determined problems, validated by the customer. Revised solutions may also emerge. These will be jointly determined solutions, endorsed at their preliminary stages by the customer. The consultative selling experience will be under way.

Once an annual plan is being implemented, your sales teams should review progress with their customers on a quarterly timetable. Are we focusing on the problems whose solutions are the most meaningful to you? Are there aspects of these problems that have become newly understood since our work began and that we should deal with? Is our solution being implemented according to plan? Should we anticipate snags in the next quarter? Are there migrations from our solution that we should be contemplating? Are there revisions or renovations that we should be considering? Is there an adjacent problem that we could also be solving simultaneously with the same solution?

The evaluation that coincides with the fourth quarter of a plan's implementation should be set aside for a combined annual review and preview meeting. What have we accomplished so far? Have we been doing what we proposed we would do? Is it working? How much incremental profit have we been able to deliver to you so far? How can we best plan the delivery of what is yet to come? Where do we go from here—what problem areas are next in line for solution? What solutions would give you the most significant results?

The review process is designed to consolidate your partnership position. You can find out where you stand based on what you have been doing. You can remind the customer of your cumulative contribution to improved profits. You can plan what comes next. By doing so, you can put yourself in position to get a head start on your forthcoming year's penetration plan and, at the same time, keep competitors out. And last but far from least, you can add the new knowledge to your data base on the customer's business that will enable you to heighten your upcoming opportunities to sell.

7
Implications and Applications

What are the implications of a key account penetration system? What can you expect when you apply it to your business?

When a business decides to serve its top customer tier from a key account penetration system, it changes more than the way it manages its principal sales strategy. It alters the nature of the sales function itself. It revises forever the relationship it shares with its major customers. And it provides a platform for taking unusually innovative approaches to the ways it goes about earning its growth profits.

Bringing the Customer In

The concept of a penetration system suggests a one-way objective, getting into customer businesses at high decision levels. In reality, the system's penetrating effects work both ways. While you are broadening and deepening your presence inside customer businesses, the customer knowledge that is being gained is flowing back into your own operations. The customer is being brought in.

Nothing more salubrious can happen to the sales function. The customer has always been its missing link. Historically, it has contained product knowledge, process knowledge, pricing knowledge, and promotional knowledge in profusion. These are all internal areas of information that have dramatized the "me-ness" of most sales functions. Rarely have they been sufficiently customer-oriented to the "they" out there. The closest to knowing about what goes on "out there" has been competitive knowledge. But even this has been more or less focused on competitive products, processes, pricing, and promotion.

A key account penetration system internalizes your customers. It brings them inside your business in the form of data about their most significant problems and opportunities that you can affect. The data do more than represent each customer. For the purposes of consultative selling, the question of what an individual customer is all about is answered by knowledge of two characteristics: the customer's problems that you can help solve and the customer's opportunities that you can help achieve.

These two shorthand ways of describing a customer are the same attributes by which your customers think of themselves. "We are these unsolved problems, and here are their costs to us. We are these unachieved opportunities, and here are their values to us. When we quantify our costs and our values, we arrive at our objectives. This is what we really are."

Bringing customers into your business means knowing their cost problems, the values they assign to their opportunities, and knowing their objectives. Their objectives are their targets. They will try to reach them by two types of strategies. One will aim to solve their cost problems. The other will seek to expand their sales opportunities. Consultative selling allows you to help them do both. But you can only help them if you know what they know.

To bring in your customers means never having to say you don't know.

When customers are inside your decision-making system, you will not be able to ignore them at the all-important initial stages of proposal, where all sales are really made. The presence of customer knowledge in your APACHE data system will affect not only your decisions but how you go about making them. "Get the customer in here"—in the form of customer data—will become your most insistent demand. Without it, you will be embarrassed at your cerebral nakedness.

Customers, no longer strangers, outsiders, or adversaries, will become familiar. You will get the feel of their businesses. Their problems and opportunities will be your starting points for selling—not your products, how they are made, or how they perform and what their price may be. All of these vendor sales points will become subservient to what you know about your customers. If they have value, it will be in relation to adding operating and financial value to your customers. If there is no value they can add, there is no value they can claim.

Diffusing Traditional Buyer-Seller Roles

When customers have been brought into your business as residents in your sales data base, and when you have penetrated their businesses in depth, breadth, and height, the traditional distinctions between buyer and seller will become diffused. Their basis, which lies in the absence of mutual objectives, will have disappeared.

Win-lose sales strategies will have no place. Because your customers must win if you are going to have a growing market, and because you must win if your customers are going to have a growing improver of their profit, your combined need for win-win relations will foster a new mutuality in your roles.

The line between selling and buying will gray out. The zone where customer interests conflict with your interests will thin down. Your need to overcome them will be converted to a need on your part to come over to their way of assigning priorities to their problems, defining the kinds of solutions they can most readily accept, and together with them, implementing the solutions inside their businesses.

You will still have to compete to serve them. But once accepted, you will become collaborators, the kind we call partners in profit. Your common objectives will be identified in your account penetration plans. Both of you will have signed off on them. The plans' strategies will also be known to both of you, approved by your customers so that they and their people can work together with you and your people to achieve your shared objectives.

In such a scenario, which is already commonplace in many key account relationships, who is buyer and who is seller—and what difference does it make? Your role will be that of a customer extender, acting as an extension of your customer's own people and their capabilities to solve the customer's problems. As an extension of customer capabilities, you can become positioned as a true adder of value. Your contribution is perceptible. It is also quantifiable.

The essence of role blending is the combined ability of you and your customer to achieve the dollar objectives of your account penetration plan. This is your pivot point in moving away from vending toward consulation. If you fail, you fall back to being a vendor. You separate out of the blend and become a supplier once again, perceived as having your own self-serving objectives that are bound to be inconsistent with the needs of your customer.

Vendors are readily identifiable as vendors, and vending is a well-accepted role. If you want to depart from it to take on a consultant positioning, the burden of proof will be on you. You must signal your new position in unmistakable terms by demonstrating that you deserve to be admitted into the special privileges that consultative sellers merit. One of these is access to top-tier managers. Another is access to top-tier information about the customers' business problems and opportunities. These are privileges not accorded to vendors. If you want to qualify for them, you must be willing to earn a partnership with your customers in the pursuit of their supreme objective—profit.

Taking a Financial Service Position

The one-to-one linkage of being positioned as a consultant to the achievement of your customers' objectives tells you exactly what your sales posture must be: You will have to sell a financial benefit. This will require you to take on aspects of a service business whose product is money, expressed in one form or another, and whose basic process is the appreciation of customer net worth. When customers have completed each of their transactions with you, they should possess a greater value than they had at the onset, even after paying your price. This is the nature of a financial service.

To the extent that the improved value of their operations is significant and consistent, they will know whether you are a good consultant with whom to do business or only an imperfectly disguised vendor.

Selling a financial benefit imposes a number of specific demands on how you train, reward, and manage a key account sales force. You will have to teach them to know enough about the effect of their products, equipment, or systems on a customer's business to be able to calculate the degree of improved value they can contribute. You will also have to teach them the language in which financial values are expressed and the fundamental arithmetic that is involved in arriving at a determination of costs, profits, breakeven points, present values, and returns on investments.

Sales representatives who sell money values and whose personal expertise is instrumental in deriving those values—both for their customers and for their own company—ought to be compensated in some proportion to the profits they improve. They can be paid a bonus on the amount of incremental profits they deliver to their accounts, for example. This will help insure the commonality of their objectives with customer objectives. To make sure that they respect the dual requirements of their mission, their bonus on customer profits can be conditioned by minimum profit returns that you expect them to earn for your own business. A kicker can be added to the bonus in cases where their achievement exceeds preset boundaries.

The act of managing a financial service sales force is principally an exercise in total commitment. You must commit yourself to prevent any relaxing of your vigilance against defining your product as consisting of what you make instead of the values from it that you sell. You must also guard against ceaseless pressures from your customers to test your commitment to consult with them rather than to vend. They will try to determine how serious you are, so they can get comfortable with their own commitment to consult with you. In addition, they will always be probing the capabilities of your sales force to bring them improved values.

A financial service sales force, more than any other, lives or dies on its ability to create measurable and attributable gains on a customer's bottom line. The gains must be guaranteed in dollar terms. The customer must be able to attribute them to you. You must be able to do it again. The customer's added profit between "before" and "after" is your "product". There is no way to hide it if it is significant. Nor is there a way to hide from it if it is not. Your emphasis on performance must therefore be unrelenting. You and your key account representatives perform in the most visible corporate fishbowl of all when you elect to sell profit. It is not that you must be more accountable than if you manage a vendor sales force. You must, though, be much more responsible to your key customers and their representatives. Without doubt, you will become the ex officio member of their relationship, acting as its maestro. You will acknowledge the basic truism of consultative selling on virtually a daily basis. A one-time failure in product performance is survivable. Profit that has been promised but does not materialize may not be.

Optimizing Key Account Contribution

The fact that a customer is a key account does not mean that all your transactions will automatically be the big-winner type that yield both of you major amounts of profits. The 80-20 rule mandates that as many as 80 percent of all transactions produce only as little as 20 percent of any key account sales team's profit contribution, either to you or to their customer. It is the remaining 20 percent that makes the key account relationship productive of growth profits.

The single most critical standard of performance for managing a key account sales force is to provide a systematic method for concentrating the time and talent of your representatives on the most productive proposals.

What composes the 80 percent, and what composes the 20 percent?

The bulk of key account transactions generally consist of proposing more or less repetitive solutions to standard, recurrent problems: improving profit by advancing the collection of receivables or by decreasing inventory carrying costs or by increasing productivity of a business function or by stepping up turnover. These problems may prevail throughout a key account's operating divisions. Or they may be epidemic only in a single division's departments. Sometimes every account in the same industry will have identical problems, because they come with the industry. To deal with them most cost-effectively, you should develop virtually standardized solutions that can be proposed, installed, and monitored in a virtually standardized manner.

Standardized solutions to standard, recurrent problems will release selling time and talent for allocation to the second category of key account sales.

Two types of situations compose this 20 percent category. One is made up of semistandardized solutions to standard problems that feature a difference from the first category: They have a one-time uniqueness about them that makes a standardized solution unworkable. The second type of situation is the custom-tailored solution. This represents the apex of your ability to apply your expertise to solve what is usually an exceptional— or once-in-a-long-time—problem of major importance to a customer's business. The custom-tailored solution must be your highest-ticket item, because it reflects the highest value that you can confer on a customer.

Custom-tailored solutions can provide multiple profit opportunities. Initially, they yield premium profits based on their premium value for the original customer. Next, they can generate additional premium profits by adaptation to closely similar problems, either with the same customer or with others in the same industry. Finally, some of them can eventually become semistandardized or standardized solutions for sale to several key accounts.

The more you can focus on selling customized solutions, the greater opportunity you will have to maximize the contribution you can make your key customers as well as the contribution you receive from them. This is the consultative version of the classic challenge of managing a sales force.

Summing Up the Key Account Mission

Bringing the customer into your key account planning will radicalize your sales performance. Once the customer is in, you can justly describe your operations as being customer-driven and market-oriented. Once in, your sales force can begin to build customer acceptance from the very start of their proposal process instead of only hoping to obtain it at the end. Once in, the connection between your customer's profits and your own will become bonded. Neither of you will ever let the other forget it.

If you accept these implications of managing major customer sales from a key account penetration system, then you will be able to take command of sales management's fundamental task: maximizing the value of your most perishable resource, the time that is available to your key account representatives to spend with their top-tier decision makers. This is "time on target," the most critical and elusive element in selling. Because it is dispensed at the pleasure of your key account customers, it cannot be bought, cajoled, or consistently manipulated. It can only be earned.

The entry and reentry price for penetrating to the top tier is the same. Your representatives must bring new learning about customer profit improvement. This is the output of their data base. They must also bring new achievement. This is the output of their proposals, aided and abetted by their data-based APACHE proposal partner. These two components of the partnering process—new learning about customer problems and new achievements in solving them—are the products of the key account penetration system.

Because it is so well prepared in advance according to customer values, to move from the penetration system into proposal is a comfortable, confidence-building experience. "For the first time," key account representatives have said, "I feel that my customers are really listening to me. And why not? It's their businesses I'm talking about, not mine. They really want me to sell, because they want the improved profits they know I can bring. As a result, it's not longer clear to me whose job I'm doing, theirs or mine. It's no longer clear to them, either. Maybe that's why we're working so well together."

Appendix 1

Superproduct Strategy for Key Account Sales to High-Growth Industries

Fast-growing industries do not necessarily have more needs than industries whose growth is slower or took place some time ago. They do, though, have more urgent needs. They require immediate benefits in order to continue their rate of growth. Their downside risk is that growth will slow, never to regain its thrust, unless problems are solved and opportunities are seized at once. For this reason, high-growth industries are often said to have "superneeds."

To provide benefits for superneeds in high-growth accounts, "superproducts" may have to be sold. A superproduct is not a single product. It is a managed package of related products, services, and systems. Its purpose is not just to offer a larger unit of sale. The main objective of a superproduct is to capture the solution to comprehensive problems that can improve customer profits quickly and on a large scale.

Superproducts offer a customer the advantages of one-stop shopping. They offer their supplier the opportunity to become a major partner. At the same time, they act to shut out competitive invasion of a key account by closing off entry points that would otherwise invite penetration.

Easing into Superproducts

What is the easiest way to construct a superproduct? At first, it might seem to be by pairing products that are complementary or supplementary. But products alone, no matter how many are assembled together, do not add up to a superproduct.

It takes service values to make a superproduct. Only services can support most products sufficiently to give them a premium operating advantage. Services are also crucial in justifying superior margins, because they enable fast-growing customers to apply products for maximum operating and financial benefits.

Services that can add the highest values to superproducts run to two types: educational and financial. The contribution of educational services is twofold. One is to help customers extract greater rewards from a superproduct's installation, operation, or maintenance. The second is to teach them how to calculate their improved rewards by computing their newly lowered costs or, more importantly to growth customers, increased sales revenues.

Financial services such as deferred payments, rental, or leasing can contribute even more fundamentally to premium price. They may make it affordable for a customer to obtain a superproduct in the first place and later to upgrade it or replace it. In the prescription of superproducts, the rule of "necessity and sufficiency" can be a useful guide. A superproduct should contain sufficient products and services to improve customer profits but only those necessary to do so.

This guideline helps protect you from the twin temptations to underengineer or overengineer a superproduct. If it is overengineered, it will probably have to be overpriced to the point where its return on the customer's investment will be significantly reduced or nullified. If it is underengineered, its performance inadequacies may contribute to customer dissatisfaction. This can invite competitive inroads. In the interests of avoiding underengineering, one or more of a superproduct's modules or service components may be obtained from other suppliers—even competitors—to round out its ability to deliver benefits.

Recognizing Common Opportunities for Superproducts

Two major types of opportunities can provide the impetus you need for the creation of superproducts for high-growth customers:

1. Customer business functions that require frequent servicing, constant monitoring, or sophisticated knowledge to operate and maintain.
2. Advances in your own technology that can produce new customer benefits.

The Dresser-Wayne superproduct is a good example of how both of these opportunities can be combined. It consists of several gas pumps and their monitoring consoles as the nucleus of the superproduct. It also contains a cash management control system, data storage and handling modems, a training program, financing options that include a lease program, and an optional architectural plan to reconstruct individual gas station configurations to maximize their throughput of customers each day. The business functions this superproduct serves require a high frequency of attention, ongoing monitoring, and include sophisticated electronics that take the place of skilled operators.

SUPERPRODUCTS TO MEET CUSTOMER NEEDS FOR ONGOING SERVICE OR NEW KNOWLEDGE

When a customer's normal use situation requires periodic servicing, replacement parts, consumables, or sophisticated operating knowledge, it is a natural candidate for a superproduct. The superproduct's hardware—its product components—may be a one-time or infrequently updated sale. The servicing it requires and its replacement parts and consumables can generate repeat sales. Over the useful life of the superproduct, repeat sales will account for its major contribution to income.

The repeat sales also provide a second benefit. They assure continuity with your key customers. They offer a valid, profit-making reason for your representatives to return again and again to sell. This gives them the opportunity to seek out new or further needs that can be supplied and upgrade the superproduct installation with more sophisticated hardware and accessories. Many superproducts include elements like these:

1. A service agreement to provide recurrent maintenance, repair, and replacement parts and consumables.
2. An educational service to teach customers how to use the superproduct. This service may involve an intensive initial teaching program supplemented by periodic refresher courses that are delivered in person or through media.

3. A turnkey operational service to provide a core of trained personnel who can act as a surrogate staff in putting the customer's superproduct to work at once.
4. A service-fee type of lease to help customers finance their superproducts.

The best type of customers are those who have been educated in a superproduct's capabilities to improve their profit. Educated customers know the full range of benefits to expect and how to achieve them. As a result, they are able to extract the highest profit contribution, because their people have a high level of operating skills. They should also have the greatest incentive to upgrade their original purchase by continually setting new and more ambitious objectives.

A superproduct's educational components must help customers maximize their understanding of its benefits. The need for smart customers is dictated by an essential fact of superproduct life: The "hardware" expense you charge your customers can generally be amortized over time; their personnel costs, however, will probably rise. The majority of dollars spent over a superproduct's life cycle go to pay its operators, not to finance its hard components. From the customers' point of view, education in cost-efficient operation is vital in extracting the full contribution you can make to their profit.

Customer education also helps improve your own profit. By teaching customers the proper operation and maintenance of your superproducts, you are taking out a form of insurance policy against undue repair bills for which you may be liable under contract. You may also be able to avoid or at least defer customer demands for service, which can come at awkward times and cause unplanned costs.

APPENDIX 1   167

For customers whose operations are governed by compliance legislation, an educational course in conforming to its controls is virtually required. Four other courses may also be included in a customer-education curriculum: operation and maintenance guidelines, profit-improvement evaluation of superproduct performance, forthcoming technological innovations that may affect a customer's operations, and finance options.

There are three basic options for superproduct financing. *Cash flow financing* is designed to pay for a superproduct and optimize your customer's cash flow at the same time. The purchase plan can be geared to a growing customer's income cycle, so that low payments can be made at first, then larger payments, and finally a third-stage drop-off. For businesses affected by seasonal cycles, a deferred or skip-payment schedule can permit smaller payments, or even no payments at all, to be made during low-income periods.

Two other financing methods are a *monthly service fee*, which is payable until the price is paid in full, and *leasing*, which permits a complete schedule of benefits to be enjoyed on a perpetual rental basis.

While these approaches differ, they share three similarities. They permit a growing customer to obtain the added values of a superproduct immediately, without waiting until they can be afforded. A series of relatively small expenditures is substituted in each case for an undigestible big lump. The option also exists for the customer to purchase at any time.

There are additional advantages to the service fee method. Because payment is extended over time, it may enable a customer to hedge against inflation. Another reason to defer payment is the possibility that you will upgrade a superproduct's performance characteristics during the life of the service fee. If this occurs, your customers can benefit at any time from your new technical developments at no additional cost.

Like service-fee financing, leasing is often an alternative to outright purchase for growing customers. Leasing is a form of rental. Under a lease, customers acquire benefits without the cost of possession. They can conserve cash and borrowing power to keep funding their growth. Leasing can be the preferred financing option whenever total dollar cost appears high, but the profit on freed capital can outweigh the cost. Leasing is also a popular option whenever asset ownership is not an advantage, as it may not be in a situation of high growth.

SUPERPRODUCTS TO MEET CUSTOMER NEEDS FOR NEW TECHNOLOGY

When technology is undergoing rapid or significant change in your industry, the creation of superproducts may confer significant benefits both to you and to your key account customers who are themselves growing from innovative technologies.

Many customers will want your new technology. Even those who want it first will be apprehensive, however. They will be beset by four reservations:

1. Reliability: Can they depend on it?
2. Capability: Will it perform?
3. Affordability: Is it cost-effective?
4. Compatibility: How does it fit in?

In order to raise their levels of comfort on these issues to the point where they will buy, a superproduct and its added educational and financial values may have to be offered. The superproduct can provide reassurance that questions of reliability and capability have been answered. Its attendant educational and financial values can help insure affordability together with compatible installation and operation.

Other customers will prefer to wait out the debugging of a new technology. A second type of superproduct can be created to meet their more conservative needs. This can take the form of a hybrid or interim product that will importantly upgrade their existing operations but will not threaten their reliability, because it will be highly compatible and more easily affordable.

Selling Superproducts by Consultation

Superproducts do not reveal their operating and financial advantage by themselves. They require an interpreter who can prove their contribution in advance of purchase. This requires two skills. One is function smartness: Each sales representative must know the costs or revenue-producing ability of the customer functions to be affected. Second, the representative must know how to quantify the dollar values by which they will be affected.

The consultative approach to superproduct sales changes more than just selling style. It also alters the nature of the product benefit: that is, of what is being sold. Superproduct selling removes the emphasis from product performance and places it on the added value of the customer's improved profits.

Of all the components in a superproduct sale, it is the key account sales representatives who can be the greatest adders of value. They scope the customer business function whose profit contribution is to be improved. They calculate the value of a problem and prescribe a solution of greater value. They define the solution in operating and financial terms. Then they structure the superproduct that will deliver the solution, manage its sale, install it, supervise and measure its performance in terms of improving customer profit, and upgrade it over time. In all of these activities, they learn more and more about the customers' business problems. At the same time, the customers learn from them more and more about your solutions. They share together in analyzing problems and measuring solutions; in other words, they consult.

In the same way that they define the superproduct they sell in financial terms rather than physically, the key account sales representatives segment their "customers." Purchasing management remains on its own tier. An upper tier is now accessible, composed of middle and top management. Because they have something to sell at upper levels—profits instead of products, new values instead of added costs, an investment instead of a cost, and a return on investment instead of an expense—their top customer tiers will be open to them.

IBM approaches the top-tier management of its key retail growth customers in a model consultative fashion on behalf of its 3660 superproduct, a computer-assisted check-out station. IBM sales representatives promote the profit-improvement benefits of reduced costs and increased sales. "For a store with gross weekly sales of $140,000, savings are projected at $7,651 a month by faster customer check-out and faster balancing of cash registers." The time required to check out an average order is said to be reduced by almost 30 percent. In addition, IBM sales representatives claim that the elimination of time and cost expenses of correcting checker errors can contribute annual savings of more than $91,000 per store.

If a store is growing, its total savings every year can approach one week's gross sales at the $140,000 level. The net value of these savings falls directly to the store's bottom line. The essential contribution made by the superproduct is to provide added growth funds that supplement the revenues from sales that can be invested for still further growth. This is the superproduct's purpose, aided and abetted in its implementation by the consultation skills of the key account sales representatives and the customer information on which they are based.

Appendix 2

Rebranding Strategy for Key Account Sales of Mature Products

At the top-tier level of a key account's management, results must be sold. There is no choice. Only results will be bought. Results are easiest to establish with products and services that can produce a demonstrably unique operating and financial result in the customer's business. We call such a product a *brand*. Because a brand can deliver a premium result, a premium price can be demanded in return.

Mature products have usually lost their ability to contribute premium results to a customer. They contribute parity results, benefits similar to those that their competitors can supply. This similarity certifies their status as commodities. Since key account sales depend so heavily on premium results, mature products may have to be *rebranded:* that is, rejuvenated with a brand's capability for providing superior operating and financial benefits.

A commodity may be rebranded in two ways. One is by going back to the drawing board for technological revamping. The other is by marketing renovation. The

decision is not either-or. Companies that choose technological change will still have to incorporate marketing
strategies alongside their new engineering.

Making Marketing Changes to Rebrand

There are four principal marketing changes to be
made before a rebranding can take place:

1. *Profit-improvement needs analysis.* You will
have to learn customer and industry norms for the business functions you affect. What are the norms for cost of
sales, and how does your customer compare? What are
profit norms on sales? Is your customer above or below
them? What is the norm for collection time on receivables, and how far above the norm is your customer?
How much money is the customer leaving on the table as
a result every year?

2. *Profit-improvement contribution analysis.* Either
by backtracking on previous applications of your product
line to customer business functions or by monitoring the
effects of prototype installations, you will have to determine each product's ability to lower a function's cost or
raise its sales revenues. This capability will then have to
be translated in terms of average profit dollars and average percentage rate of return on investment. These averages will provide ballpark guidelines for the specific
values you will have to come up with for each function's
improved profit contribution within each customer account.

3. *Systems protection.* You may have to add value
to your product by packaging it into a system that will
surround it with complementary products and services
that can be sold as a single cost-reducing or sales-
increasing unit. The system's combined price can then be

presented as an investment. Its profit-improvement capability can be shown as the return on the investment.

4. *Consultative selling.* Your key account sales force will have to be trained to sell the system's rate of return to customers—not the product and service system that produces it or the mature product that has been incorporated into the system.

The essential difference between consultative selling of a rebranded product or system and the vendor selling of commodity products can be dramatized in this way:

A product-driven commodity sales representative in the chemicals business sells "pounds" to customers by saying: "Our product will solve your formulation problem. It is safe, effective, high in quality, in good supply, and available at competitive prices. We provide free application services to help you insure the solution."

A consultative representative in the same industry makes a very different approach, even though the product is completely undifferentiated: "Your formulation functions can be reduced in their yearly cost to you by $50,000. In return for a one-time $100,000 investment, you can expect a first-year saving of $50,000 and an annual saving thereafter of $50,000. This gives you payback in two years and adds $50,000 to your profit every year for as long as your formulation process remains the same."

In the first instance, a mature product is being sold on its comparative technical specifications and the performance benefits that can be derived from them. Since competition has matched them, one of two things must happen. Either increasingly finite distinctions must be painstakingly explained by the representative, raising the cost of every sale, or the price must be progressively lowered, reducing the representative's margins.

In the second instance, the customer's investment

and the amount and flow of the return it will yield are being used as the basis for a purchase decision. The product remains a commodity. By rebranding its benefits, it can be sold at a premium price.

Rebranding One of the World's Largest Companies

In the late 1960s, AT&T was catapulted by legislative fiat from monopolistic utility into the competitive marketplace. In common with most utilities, AT&T strength had been in providing reactive service, not in campaigning for aggressive sales. Its market knowledge was weak. It knew its customers in terms of their peculiar arrays of wiring installations, but not as businesses with problems that could be solved by the application of telecommunications technology. It was organized along operating lines, not according to end-user markets. Its monopoly position had allowed the company to control the rate of obsolescence for its products and to commercialize new technology as management, not the market, decreed. As a result, the majority of its outstanding hardware was composed of mature products.

Within a short period of time, this mature inventory was in key account competition with IBM, ITT, and GTE as well as with young, dynamic marketers whose technology was responsive to market needs and whose prices were lower. Under this type of pincers attack, AT&T turned to three strategies to preserve, and to grow, the commercial and industrial business sector of its multibillion-dollar annual revenue stream.

1. *Industry-need specialization.* As a utility, AT&T had segmented its markets according to customer size: small general businesses or major users. Today, market segmentation is based on industry needs to use telecom-

munications technology for reducing operating costs or
for increasing sales revenues. In each segment, AT&T
has come to recognize that its single most important
growth resource is its industry information base on
where customer costs can be reduced and how customer
sales revenues can be improved.

   2. *Industry-by-industry positioning*. By applying its
knowledge of industry costs and sales opportunities that
can be affected by telecommunications, AT&T is attempting to gain a position as each industry's preferred
"profit-improving problem solver." The company's main
approach to customers is financial. The problems for
which it prescribes, installs, and monitors solutions are
considered solved only when customer profits have been
improved.

   Key account managers and their marketing, technical, and information teams are being taught to carry out a
three-step sales procedure with customers: (1) Identify a
problem and quantify its effect; (2) quantify the effect of
the most cost-effective system to solve the problem; (3)
sell the dollars-and-cents effect as representing the value
added by AT&T. A simplified case story will illustrate
the consultative selling approach.

   A typical problem that can be solved by communica-
tions technology is a sluggish accounts receivable process that deprives a customer of access to cash flow. In
one customer, AT&T discovered that four separate functions—billing, accounting, sales, and legal—were involved
in past-due collections. Twenty-two separate steps, each
adding costs, were necessary to collect many receivables. Others were never collected. The average annual
earnings loss on receivables outstanding more than 30
days was $1.75 million. This was the customer's true cost
of its collection system.

   To solve the problem, AT&T prescribed a telemar-

keting collection system. The customer's annual investment is about $350,000. The net annual saving to the
customer is $1.4 million, all of which can be brought
down to the bottom line as the increased annual profit
contributed by AT&T.

   3. *Return-on-investment sales consultation.* AT&T
has taken on the new posture of consulting on the improvement of its customers' profit, not simply supplying
them with hardware and technological know-how. Customers are no longer being asked to spend money, incur
costs, or lease equipment. Instead, sales presentations
are adopting the style of financial plans that document a
positive return on the customers' investment. A system
becomes valued by a customer according to the ROI it
will deliver, not the cost of the mature products from
which it has been assembled.

Creating a Rebranding Doctrine

   Rebranding defies the law of business gravity: Products that descend into maturity can rarely be rejuvenated. This has become unwritten doctrine in many
long-established companies. If rebranding is to become a
key account sales strategy, it will have to be committed
to a written doctrine that will have the force of a sales
policy statement.
   A rebranding doctrine such as the one shown here
can play a powerful teaching and motivating role by its
treatment of three key subject areas. One seeks agreement on the purpose of rebranded businesses, so that
their contribution to growth profits will be understood
and accepted. A second subject explains the premium
pricing capability of rebranded products. The third subject fixes an irreplaceable role for key account selling as

the prime strategy that educates customers about the nature and dimension of the added value in which they will be asked to invest.

Rebranding Doctrine

1. The principal objective of key account sales is to grow incremental profits.
2. The principal means of growing incremental profits is to obtain premium price.
3. The basis for premium price is the ability to deliver premium value.
4. A rebranded product's price is based on the value of the customer's return on the investment needed to acquire the added value.
5. The principal capability for rebranding is knowledge of how customer costs can be reduced and how sales can be increased.

Rebranding can move more than products. It moves top-tier selling to the forefront of corporate disciplines. By doing so, it moves companies in their role as suppliers closer to their sources of funds, their customers.

Appendix 3

Market-Centering Strategy for Key Account Sales to Dedicated Markets

There is no substitute for market dedication as the source of profit growth from sales. Market dedication means focusing resources on specific markets that are the core of your profit contribution. The best way to accomplish this resource focus is to build it into the organizational structure of your business, so that your major markets become the centers around which your key account sales take place.

Companies that adopt top-tier selling as a way of life are increasingly organizing around their key markets instead of around their product or processing capabilities.

IBM has organized its operations according to its key markets, such as institutions like hospitals and retail establishments like supermarkets. Xerox Information Systems Group, which sells copiers and duplicators, has converted from geographical selling to vertical selling by industry. Even the strict technical-processing orientation of some scientific companies is giving way to a combined product and market orientation. In its electronics product marketing, Hewlett-Packard has created a sales and

service group that concentrates separately on the electri-
cal manufacturing market, while another group serves
the market for aerospace. Still other groups concentrate
their sales exclusively on the markets for communica-
tions or transportation equipment.

General Electric has constructed market-centered
business groups for its major appliance and power-
generation businesses. For GE, the process of reorganiz-
ing from a product to a market orientation has been
especially difficult. An average department contained
three and one-half product lines and served more than
one business or, more frequently, only a part of a major
business. Electric motors, for example, were divided
among eight departments. Home refrigerators were split
between two departments, even though the only
significant product difference was the way the doors
open. In such a setup, department managers understand-
ably became oriented to specific product lines rather than
to the needs of a total market.

In other companies, a wide range of businesses are
being centered in one fashion or another on their markets. At Mead, broad market clusters serve customer
needs in home building and furnishings, education, and
leisure. Monsanto has organized a Fire Safety Center
that consolidates fire-protection products from every
sector of the company and groups them according to the
market they serve: building and construction, transportation, apparel, or furnishings. Revlon has been engaged in
"breaking up the company into little pieces": Six autono-
mous profit centers are each designed to serve a specific
market segment.

PPG Industries has been examining the benefits of
systemizing the sales of its paint, ceramics, and glass
divisions through a Home Environment Center. The center's product mix could look like this:

Interior Protection and Performance Group
   Glass doors.
   Ceramic kitchen countertops and work
      surfaces.
   Interior household paints.

Exterior Protection and Performance Group
   Glass doors, windows, and window walls.
   Ceramic poolside and picnic areas.
   Exterior household paints.

By making a market the center of a sales organization's focus instead of a product, a process, or a region,
banks have been serving the common financial needs of
manufacturers of electronics systems with a dedicated
key account sales force. Another separate sales force
calls on drug and cosmetics accounts. Still another sells
financial sources to household product makers.

Benefits of Market Centering

Defining your business according to your key customer markets by organizing to serve comprehensive
sets of their needs with dedicated sales groups can produce several major benefits:

1. A market center forms a natural supply center.
The sales and distribution of all the products and services
your company makes that can be used by the same market are centralized with a single sales organization.

2. A market center insures that customers will be
required to deal only with its representative to gain access to the sum total of your company's product lines
and services.

3. A market center permits the key account sales
representatives and their support teams who are dedi-

cated to a single industry to become unusually well versed in knowing its people, problems, and the customer processes into which they must sell your products.

4. A market center provides a ready-made environment for an APACHE-type industry data base on its problems and opportunities that you can solve.

5. A market center allows its customer to identify you as a premier source of supply that specializes in solving their unique problems. This creates a predisposed opportunity for you to develop an institute approach to your market by acting as its chief information center and educator as well as marketer.

Guidelines for Market Centering

If you are currently centering your key account sales operations around one or more product lines, the manufacturing processes that make them, or the geographical territories in which your customers do business, three guidelines will help you to market center:

1. A market center must be chartered to serve a market that is defined according to closely related needs. This permits the market to be served by a diversified system of products and services that, taken together, supply a combination of closely related benefits. The market center may sell two or more related products in a single sale or sell a system composed of products and their related services.

2. Because a market center is operated as a profit center, it should be administered by an industry sales manager. Unlike product managers or brand managers, or even market managers who are merely profit-accountable, industry sales managers are responsible for both profit and volume. They enjoy considerable author-

ity in running their businesses. They command the key decisions. They set prices, control costs, and are charged with operating their market centers for a satisfactory profit on sales.

3. Once a key account sales group is market-centered, its storehouse of market information becomes its key asset. Through market centering, an industry information center can be set up to store and give broad industrywide access to its market knowledge on a fee basis.

Two case histories will illustrate how these guidelines have been implemented by two very different corporations, NCR and General Foods, in order to achieve a similar objective: to have a single sales representative be able to serve all or most of each key customer's needs in the industry of the representative's dedication.

THE NCR APPROACH

NCR has organized its traditional product-line sales approach into a strategy of "selling by vocation" on an industry-by-industry basis. Each vocation is a broad industry grouping that forms a specific market definable by reasonably cohesive needs. NCR is focusing a separate sales force on each of the following vocational markets: financial institutions, retailers, commercial and industrial businesses, and computer customers in medical, educational, and government offices.

NCR's market-centered sales organization enables the company to be more competitive, especially in the marketing of systems. In each market, the NCR key account sales representative assigned to it can sell coordinated systems of numerical recording and sorting products. Previously, each sales representative could sell only one divisional or departmental product line. As a result, a customer decision maker could be involved with several NCR sales representatives. No one of them could possibly know the sum total of the customer's numerical control needs, let alone be able to serve them. Under the market-centered approach, the same retail industry sales representative who sells an NCR cash register to a department store can also search out and serve the store's needs for NCR accounting machines, data entry terminals, and a mainframe computer. If the representative needs help, he or she can organize a team with other NCR representatives that can bring the required strength to a proposal. The product groups the representative sells are still manufactured separately. The centralized sales approach is the innovation that makes the difference.

By selling systems of products through a single sales representative or sales team, rather than selling individual products through many uncoordinated representatives, NCR believes it is helping its key customers achieve greater profit improvement. It can prescribe systems that solve comprehensive problems that would otherwise remain immune to single-product solutions. Sales management also believes it can expand its profitable sales volume by selling larger packages and insulating its position against competition.

Each vocational market center's full range of recording and sorting needs is becoming better known to NCR. In turn, by specializing in seeking out and serving these needs, each of NCR's vocational sales organizations is becoming known for expertise in its market, almost as if it were an independent specialist company. Moreover, every sales group can utilize the total financial and technical resources of the company for professional counsel and support in developing, prescribing, and installing product systems.

The General Foods Approach

Whereas NCR was motivated to market center by the increasing preferences of its customers for systems and by the relentless competitive pressures of IBM, General Foods revised its approach because of internal strains and frustrations. In the early 1970s, new product winners either stopped coming out of product development at their former rate or carried an unreasonable cost. Better knowledge of the needs of its consumers was obviously required if the company's product developers were to harmonize their technologies with the new lifestyles influencing the demand for processed foods. At the same time, the needs of the company's customers at the retail level required new responses. Competitive brands were proliferating, clamoring for shelf and display space. An increasingly attractive profit on sales was making private-label products more acceptable to the major supermarket chains.

These events combined to place unprecedented strains on the company's divisional structure, which was the legacy of a generations-old policy of acquisition. General Foods' major food divisions—BirdsEye, Jell-O, Post, and Kool-Aid—had evolved historically, each according to the process technology that it brought into the company. As the scope of each division's product categories grew, it was inevitable that one division's consumer provinces would be impinged on by other divisions, and that any given market would be served in a fragmented rather than a concentrated manner. Divisional sovereignties frequently made it impossible for the company to dominate a market that was served by two or more divisions with related product categories but with different styles and degrees of commitment.

Often more damaging for new-product development was the way in which division managers respected a no-man's-land between their provinces. This left gaps in product categories that gave competitors a clear shot. Even when they missed, the gaps prevented General Foods from establishing a position of undeniable category leadership.

The General Foods approach to market centering has been to reorganize its process-oriented division structure into separate selling organizations. Each market center concentrates on selling families of products made by different processing technologies but consumed by the same market segment. The Dessert Food Center, for example, coordinates the sales strategy for all desserts, whether they are frozen, powdered, or ready-to-eat. The Breakfast Foods center sells breakfast drinks made from three different processing technologies. The Pet Food Center sells dog foods, regardless of whether they come from freeze-dried, dry pellet, or semimoist processes.

Dessert Food Center
   Powdered mixes
   Frozen
   Canned ready-to-eat

Breakfast Food Center
   Powdered beverage mixes
   Frozen
   Canned ready-made

Pet Food Center
   Dry pellet
   Semimoist
   Freeze-dried

This approach of centering entire product families on a market relates the sales organization closely to the needs of the company's retail customers and end-user consumers. Each market center functions like a miniature division. It draws on the full range of corporate technologies and support services such as market research, production, and new-product development. Its primary mission is to capture its market by concentrating the corporation's complete range of resources against it.

Obtaining Support Services Under Market Centering

Market centering decentralizes the management of key account sales. On the other hand, it centralizes many of the support services that industry sales managers and their key account sales representatives must use. Four groups of service functions are consolidated in many market-centered organizations

Development services combine new-market research and development with new-product R&D under a single director. In this way, the market orientation of R&D—historically one of the chief stumbling blocks in raising a company's level of responsiveness to its customers—is accomplished organizationally. New-market needs, new-process technology, and new-product development are able to interact harmoniously rather than competitively. With market centering, the traditional vice-presidential functions for marketing and R&D can be subsumed under the director of development's functions.

Control services take on the basic research to evaluate the effectiveness of established product and service-system marketing. They also provide the necessary recruitment, compensation and motivation, training and development, legal, and financial functions. *Production services* coordinate engineering and manufacturing operations. And *promotion services* combine sales, advertising, and publicity.

Two-Way Growth Opportunity

Market centering may come to rank in importance with Alfred Sloan's decentralization of General Motors along market-segmented lines. Market-centered companies see themselves regaining a customer focus that often became blurred by Procter & Gamble's brand management system. While contemporary with Sloan's market awareness, brand management directed the styles of many corporate formats away from customers and back to products. When product and brand management were imposed on the traditional manufacturing division and on the pyramid type of organization, which was adapted for the needs of commercial business from Von Moltke's general staff concept, progress toward market centering slowed for half a century.

In the mid-1960s, the beginning of a new thrust toward the customer was signaled by the advent of free-form marketing groups. They were allowed to cut across corporate pyramids whenever unusual market sensitivity was demanded in an operation. A variety of problem-solving task forces and project management teams came into being for much the same reason; they represented jerry-built improvisations to defeat a product-oriented or process-centered organizational system.

Market centering a business can give it a two-way flexibility. Each of its major markets can be sold to more intensively once it is established as the center of a business. The same market can be sold to more extensively as well. Its related needs can be sought out and served along with the primary needs you are already meeting. This will provide you with a two-lane avenue for accelerated sales growth.

Index

account, key, *see* key account
account continuity, maintaining,
    108–111
action partners, 23
advertising and sales promotion,
    as component of marketing,
    32–33
advocate-type partners, 23
alliance(s)
    collaborative strategy for, 49
    contract, 62–64
    education strategy for, 49
    financial improvement to de-
      velop, 42
    with financial management,
      46–47
    with functional management,
      46–47
    importance of, 42
    insuring continuity of, 58–62
    migration plans, 64
    negotiate strategy for, 49–50
    objectives of, 48–50
    operational improvement to
      develop, 43–44
    with partners, 50–51
    people improvement to de-
      velop, 42–43
    with purchasing management,
      47–48
    rules for, 52–54
    with top management, 41–44

    see also departnering, partner-
      ship(s)
annual reports, as customer
    source, 83
APACHE (Account Penetration
    at Customer High levels of
    Entry)
    in consultative selling, x
    and customer mix optimizing,
      138–140
    data system, 5–6, 9
    and Dresser-Wayne, 101–102
    as multiplier, 118
    and penetration monitoring,
      106
    as proposal partner, 22, 24–25
    and time ratios, 96

bottom-tier selling
    as price selling, *vii*
    sales volume in, *viii*
business
    financial service, 7–8
    product-defined, 6
business function(s)
    as consultation subject, 66
    evaluation of, 68–69
    intensity of, 69–71
    knowledge, use of, 89–90
    as problem source, 65
    profile of, 66–67
    remedies for, 68–69